Intermittent Fasting 16/8:

The Effective Weight Loss Guide for Women and Men Wanting to Fast, Burn Fat, and Activate Autophagy While Still Enjoying Delicious Meals

© Copyright 2021

The contents of this book may not be reproduced, duplicated or transmitted without direct written permission from the author.

Under no circumstances will any legal responsibility or blame be held against the publisher for any reparation, damages, or monetary loss due to the information herein, either directly or indirectly.

Legal Notice:

You cannot amend, distribute, sell, use, quote or paraphrase any part or the content within this book without the consent of the author.

Disclaimer Notice:

Please note the information contained within this document is for educational and entertainment purposes only. No warranties of any kind are expressed or implied. Readers acknowledge that the author is not engaging in the rendering of legal, financial, medical or professional advice. Please consult a licensed professional before attempting any techniques outlined in this book.

By reading this document, the reader agrees that under no circumstances are is the author responsible for any losses, direct or indirect, which are incurred as a result of the use of information contained within this document, including, but not limited to, —errors, omissions, or inaccuracies.

Contents

- CONTENTS 5
- INTRODUCTION 1
- CHAPTER 1: THE SCIENCE OF FASTING 4
  - HISTORY OF FASTING 5
  - UNDERSTANDING THE "FASTED" AND "FED" STATES OF THE BODY 6
- CHAPTER 2: WHAT IS INTERMITTENT FASTING 16/8? 9
  - THE 16/8 PROTOCOL 9
  - CELLULAR CHANGES 11
  - MYTHS ABOUT INTERMITTENT FASTING 13
- CHAPTER 3: THE BENEFITS OF FASTING 18
  - REGULATES BLOOD SUGAR LEVELS 18
  - TACKLES INFLAMMATION 19
  - STABILIZES BLOOD PRESSURE AND CHOLESTEROL LEVELS ... 20
  - IMPROVES COGNITIVE FUNCTIONING 20
  - PROMOTES WEIGHT LOSS 21
  - STIMULATES METABOLISM 21
  - REDUCES THE RISK OF CANCER 22
  - KICK-STARTS AUTOPHAGY 23
  - EASILY SUSTAINABLE 23

CHAPTER 4: WHAT TO KNOW BEFORE FASTING 25
Who Shouldn't Try Fasting? 25
Considerations before Fasting 27

CHAPTER 5: UNDERSTANDING WEIGHT LOSS DIFFERENCES BETWEEN MEN AND WOMEN 30
Understanding Body Metabolism 30
Weight Loss in Men and Women 33

CHAPTER 6: HOW TO EXERCISE WHILE FASTING 36
Exercise Options 37
Exercise Tips 38

CHAPTER 7: BEGINNING THE 16/8 FASTING DIET 42
What to Eat During the Fasting Window 42
How to Break a Fast 45
What to Eat Right after Breaking the Fast 46
Basic Dietary Suggestions 48
Getting Started with Intermittent Fasting 51

CHAPTER 8: HOW TO KEEP MOTIVATED WHILE FASTING 55
Make a List of Your Goals 55
Have an Accountability Partner 56
Establish Short-Term Goals 57
Inspiring Content 57
The Carrot and the Stick 58
Creative Visualization 59
Focus on the Positives 60
Be Compassionate 60
Check Your Progress 61

CHAPTER 9: NON-SCALE VICTORIES AND FASTING SETBACKS 62
Non-Scale Victories to Celebrate 62
Fasting Setbacks to Tackle 66

CHAPTER 10: INTERMITTENT FASTING 16/8 RECIPES AND MEAL PLAN 72

- MEAL SHAKES 72
  - Peanut Butter Cup Shake 72
  - Dark Chocolate Peppermint Shake 74
  - Strawberry Cheesecake Shake 75
  - Very Berry Super Shake 76
  - Pineapple Green Smoothie 77
  - Strawberry Chocolate Smoothie 78
  - Carrot Apple Smoothie 79
  - Mango Raspberry Smoothie 80
  - Strawberry Oat Smoothie 81
  - Raspberry Peanut Butter Smoothie 82
  - Flax Seed Smoothie 83
- BREAKFAST RECIPES 84
  - Veggie Mini Quiches 84
  - Ham, Egg, and Avocado Breakfast Burrito 86
  - Cauliflower English Muffins 87
  - Broccoli and Parmesan Cheese Omelet 89
  - Summer Skillet Vegetable and Egg Scramble 91
  - Loaded Baked Potato Breakfast Casserole 93
  - Layered Chia Pudding with Mixed Fruit Puree 95
  - Choco-Chip and Banana Pancakes 97
  - Sweet Potato Waffles 99
- **PINK BREAKFAST BOWL** 100
  - Chocolate Fudge Brownie Oatmeal 101
- LUNCH RECIPES 102
  - Black Beans and Mango Salad 102
  - Green Goddess Salad with Chicken 103
  - Cucumber Turkey Club Sandwich 105
  - Tuna and Chickpea Pita Sandwiches 106
  - Egg Salad Lettuce Wraps 108
  - Cabbage Barley Soup 110

- Carolina Shrimp Soup 111
- Sesame Shrimp with Smashed Cucumber Salad 113
- Quinoa Corn Chowder 115
- Oven-Fried Chicken 117
- Greek Salad Wraps 119

SNACK RECIPES 120
- Mini Chicken Fajitas 120
- Hummus 122
- Easy Oven Baked Falafel 123
- Apple Pie Energy Bites 125
- Chipotle Black Bean Dip with Corn Chips 127
- Almond Poppy Crackers 129
- Frozen Berry Yogurt 131
- Turkey Pesto Roll-Up 132
- Tomato Basil Soup 133
- Zucchini Feta Fritters 134

DINNER RECIPES 136
- Mediterranean Meatballs Gyro Sandwich 136
- Turkey Chili 139
- Chicken Chow Mein 141
- Chicken Tortilla Soup 143
- Maple Glazed Salmon 145
- Vegetarian Bourguignon 146
- Vegetarian Enchilada Casserole 148
- Ham and Pineapple Rice 150
- Skillet Chicken Parmesan 151
- Skillet Lasagna 153

SAMPLE MEAL PLAN 155

CONCLUSION 157

HERE'S ANOTHER BOOK BY DARON MCCLAIN THAT YOU MIGHT LIKE 159

REFERENCES 160

Introduction

Our modern lifestyle is all about convenience and comfort. These two factors also influence what foods we consume and what diets we follow. Most of us don't pay much attention to what we eat or when we eat, which seems to be the primary cause of steadily increasing health problems. The simplest way to remedy all this is by becoming mindful of your diet. Since there are countless diets to choose from, how do you know which one will work best for you? Well, you don't have to look any further because intermittent fasting is for anyone!

The concept of fasting is not new or foreign, and humans have been fasting since time immemorial. Fasting gives your body a much-needed breather to stabilize its internal systems and functions. Intermittent fasting is a protocol that alternates between periods of eating and fasting. It is a great, simple way to optimize your overall health and wellbeing. From weight loss and maintenance to improving heart health, energy levels, and metabolism, there is a lot to gain from it.

You can do all this while enjoying delicious meals. Yes, you read that right! Dieting is no longer synonymous with eating measly portions or starving.

Intermittent fasting is perfectly sustainable in the long run. The 16/8 protocol is one of the most popular forms of intermittent fasting. You essentially fast for sixteen hours daily while the eating window is restricted to eight hours on this diet. During these eight hours, you can consume three healthy, wholesome, and delicious meals. By becoming mindful of your diet, paying attention to the food choices you make, and adding a little exercise to your daily life, you can achieve your weight loss and fitness goals. This is a great way to quickly burn fat by engaging your body's metabolism.

This book will teach you the meaning of intermittent fasting, how it works, and the various benefits it offers. The 16/8 intermittent fasting protocol is quite easy to follow and can be readily adjusted according to your preferences and lifestyle. This book contains plenty of practical tips you can follow to transition to this diet effortlessly. It also contains steps to improve your chances of success and a few common intermittent fasting mistakes you need to avoid. Apart from that, this book also includes a detailed guide of what you can and cannot eat while following this diet, how to break your fast, and what you can consume during the fasting period.

In all aspects of life, motivation is important, and dieting is no different. By following the simple suggestions in this book on staying motivated and tackling fasting setbacks, your chances of success are bound to increase. You will also learn tips to help you add exercise to your daily routine, and gain an understanding of how your metabolism affects your ability to gain or lose weight. All in all, this book will act as your transitional guide toward intermittent fasting.

Lastly, this book includes several 16/8 intermittent fasting recipes and a detailed meal plan to help get you started. All the recipes in this book are super nutritious and incredibly simple to prepare without compromising taste or flavor. You need not worry about counting calories to lose weight. Simply pay attention to *when* you eat—this is the only change you need to make. Forget about spending hours in the kitchen cooking diet-friendly meals. Once you start cooking the suggested recipes in this book, your idea of cooking will change for the better. Following a diet has never been this easy and accessible. Or this fun!

Chapter 1: The Science of Fasting

Most health problems we face nowadays are primarily caused by our modern diets. This is where fasting steps in. As a time-tested ancient tradition, fasting has been a part of human life since time immemorial. Whether for spiritual or medical reasons, fasting is quite a common practice.

One of the biggest misconceptions people have about fasting is that it is synonymous with starvation. Unless you change your mindset about fasting, you cannot make it a part of your daily lifestyle. The difference is that starvation is involuntary and is caused by the absence of food. In contrast, fasting is a deliberate, conscious, and therefore controlled act. You never know where your next meal will come from or when you can eat again with starvation. When voluntarily abstaining from consuming any solid foods, this is known as fasting. Fasting is not only natural but steadily gaining popularity in health and fitness communities worldwide.

History of Fasting

Fasting is an ancient healing tradition practiced by most cultures and religions across the globe. Hippocrates, considered to be the father of modern science, was a staunch proponent of regular fasting. A common treatment he prescribed was fasting and consuming apple cider vinegar on an empty stomach to promote one's health. He believed that eating while sick merely makes the illness fester. Plutarch, an ancient Greek writer and historian, had similar sentiments. He believed that it is best to make fasting a part of your daily life instead of depending on medicine and treatment. Other famous Greek thinkers such as Plato and Aristotle also backed these claims. They all believed fasting could be used as prevention and cure.

This goes to show how ancient Greeks believed medical treatment and options could be inspired by nature. In fact, most animals don't usually eat when they're sick; this is one reason why fasting is labeled as "the physician within your body." It is the basic instinct that makes animals such as cats or dogs effectively anorexic when sick. However, it is not just animals. Even humans experience reduced appetite when they are unwell. Take a moment and think about it: back when you were sick with the flu, you probably realized that eating was the last thing on your mind. Even foods you normally crave suddenly seem unappetizing when you're sick. This is your body's way of inducing an automatic fast to heal itself. The human body is quite intuitive, and it usually knows what it needs to heal and repair itself. Fasting is a part of our human instinct and is deeply embedded into our biological heritage. Sadly, though, most of us ignore these cues and treat our bodies as tireless machines.

Another popular belief about fasting is that it can help improve your cognitive abilities. If you take a moment and think about it, it makes perfect sense. How do you feel after a heavy and greasy meal made up of carbs and sugars? Chances are you feel quite tired and sluggish. You certainly do not feel energetic. Reduction in your energy levels and sluggishness are both associated with the heavy food you consume. Most of your body's blood supply is directed to the digestive system after a heavy meal to digest the food you have just consumed. This, in turn, reduces the blood supply available to other organs, especially the brain. This results in lethargy and drowsiness. You are essentially inducing your body into a state of "food coma" by eating heavy meals. When you start fasting regularly, this process is reversed.

Aside from fasting for health reasons, fasting is also widely considered a spiritual practice. It is commonly practiced in many religions and cultures across the globe. Whether in Hinduism, Islam, Christianity, Judaism, Jainism, or Buddhism, fasting is a sacred practice. It is used as a means for spiritual enlightenment and purification. Several religious scriptures suggest fasting has healing powers. It is also believed to purge your soul of all sins you may have committed. Another popular religious notion holds that fasting helps connect your body, mind, and soul.

During the holy month of Ramadan, Muslims fast from sunrise until sunset. Islamic scriptures suggest fasting twice a week is good for your body and soul. Likewise, Buddhist monks are known for observing strict fasts quite frequently. Even Hindu scripture describes similar notions. So, it is safe to say that fasting is not a modern concept and has managed to stand the test of time.

Understanding the "Fasted" and "Fed" States of the Body

There are several misconceptions about fasting, which we now know are myths. Fasting does not harm your body. To understand how it works, you need to differentiate between the two primary states of the human body: "fasted" and "fed" states. Your body is in either of these states at all times. It cannot be in both states simultaneously.

Humans have evolved and all the amenities, innovations, and technology at our disposal have made our lives rather convenient. Convenience and choice are two characteristics of the modern lifestyle. This is especially true for our diet these days. Walk into any grocery store, and you will see multiple options. When so many snacks and food options are available, constant snacking has become the norm. Most of us are used to snacking on something or other throughout the day. Whenever you eat, your body is in a fed state. In this state, your body primarily focuses on the digestion, absorption, and assimilation of the food you consume.

As you eat, the food is transformed into energy by your body's internal metabolism. All of this energy is not immediately used, and a portion of it is stored for later. This is a part of our evolutionary mechanism to ensure survival. All the energy in reserve is like your body's personal savings account. Your body dips into this reserve only when there is a shortage of food. This extra energy is stored in the form of fat cells. Since there is no upper limit to the number of fat cells that can be created, your body is equipped to accumulate as much fat as it wants to. This process continues for as long as your body is in a fed state.

On the other hand, a fasted state is one where you abstain from eating, either voluntarily or involuntarily. Your body utilizes those fat reserves during the fasted state. When you don't eat, your body has nothing to do other than depend on its energy resources to keep itself going. Most of us are in a fasted state only when we are sleeping. Think of fasting as a simple extension of this period: as long as you eat, you are in a fed state, and when you stop eating, you are in a fasted state.

A primary law of nature is that there needs to be balance. This is embodied through the Chinese philosophy of Yin and Yang, which symbolizes the importance of balance. This balance is crucial in all aspects of your life, which is the root cause of most problems. This applies to your body, too. If you want your body to function efficiently and effectively, there must be a balance between fasted and fed states. If you are constantly in either of these states, it will harm your health and wellbeing in the long run. The simplest way to ensure that this balance exists is through fasting.

Chapter 2: What is Intermittent Fasting 16/8?

Intermittent fasting is incredibly versatile. While following intermittent fasting, you can fast daily, on alternate days, or adjust the fasting protocol according to your needs and requirements. The most popular form of intermittent fasting is the 16/8 diet, also known as the 16:8 fasting diet or the lean gains method. This method of intermittent fasting was popularized by a trainer called Martin Berkhan. Here's a fun fact: did you know that Hugh Jackman followed the lean gains approach to achieve his famous Wolverine physique?

The 16/8 Protocol

This simple intermittent fasting protocol requires you to fast for sixteen hours daily. This automatically reduces the eating window to eight hours. If you take a moment and think about it, your body is regularly in a fasted state. Are you wondering how this happens? Well, as mentioned, your body is essentially fasting when you are asleep. Think of the 16/8 protocol as a mere extension of this fasted state. Perhaps the primary benefit of this form of intermittent fasting is its simplicity.

Most of us have busy lives and rushed mornings. If you are no stranger to skipping breakfast, this method will be quite easy to follow. It suggests that you fast for sixteen consecutive hours. According to your needs and requirements or convenience, you can change the fasting window. For instance, if you are comfortable with the idea of skipping breakfast or are used to doing this, then your first meal will be at noon and the last meal at eight in the evening. Do you see what happened here? You are automatically fasting for sixteen hours, and the eating window is restricted to eight hours. This is just one example of the lean gains protocol.

As mentioned earlier, you can customize the fast according to your obligations, lifestyle, and more. Let's say, if you like the idea of waking up early in the morning and exercising, you can reschedule the eating window to accommodate your nutritional needs after working out. For instance, you can wake up early in the morning, exercise, have your first meal at around 10 a.m. and the last at 6 p.m. As long as the eating window is restricted to eight hours, you can change the fasting schedule. This is entirely up to you. Intermittent fasting is not a restrictive diet; the only thing you need to pay attention to is when you eat.

During the eating window, you can consume three wholesome and healthy meals. You can also consume non-caloric foods and beverages during that window. As long as you don't over-compensate during the eating window by consuming unhealthy meals, you can achieve all the benefits of intermittent fasting. By following this protocol, your calorie intake will automatically be reduced. It also makes you more conscious about your eating patterns and dietary choices. A little extra attention and conscious effort are all it takes to achieve your weight loss and fitness goals. You will learn more in the upcoming chapters.

Cellular Changes

Now that you understand what intermittent fasting is, you need to understand how the process works on a cellular level. Several changes take place in your body while fasting. Your body is similar to a machine. All machines suffer from wear and tear when used regularly. Certain parts of the machine need to be replaced, the oil has to be changed, and it needs regular servicing. What happens to the machine without regular upkeep? Sooner or later, it will stop functioning. This is what happens to your body, too. A common mistake most of us make is we treat our bodies like tireless machines. To be fair, even machines need maintenance; the best way to improve your body's function is through intermittent fasting.

This dietary protocol triggers certain helpful changes at a cellular level through a process known as autophagy. In simple terms, autophagy is a natural process and is similar to regular servicing. It is triggered when your body is under stress; the word stress here doesn't have any negative connotations. Instead, it refers to the stress induced on the body during fasting when it needs to dip into its internal reserves of energy to keep functioning. Autophagy helps repair and replace damaged cells. In autophagy, your body starts to cannibalize all the old and defunct cells. It might sound morbid, but this is an incredibly helpful process. Without autophagy, there would be a buildup of defunct and malfunctioning cells in the body, which can hinder your overall wellbeing. This process is also known to remove the buildup of toxins. In a way, autophagy is like your body's housekeeping service; only when the damaged cells are removed or repaired can your body start to generate healthier ones. It helps detoxify your body from the inside.

Another essential cellular change pertains to the stabilization of blood sugar levels. Over the past few decades, diabetes has become a global health problem for millions of people. It is characterized by low levels of insulin and high levels of blood sugar. Your body produces the insulin hormone whenever you eat anything to process the food and convert it into glucose. Glucose levels in the blood increase when your body cannot produce sufficient insulin or if there's a resistance to it. All this is done away with when you don't eat anything. If you don't consume any food, your body doesn't have to produce insulin. It means you are reducing any fluctuations in blood sugar levels. As such, fasting may help reverse the effects of type-2 diabetes, however, always seek medical advice before trying any new diet, since people with diabetes may be at risk of hypoglycemia and hyperglycemia.

The human growth hormone (HGH) is crucial in regulating the body's metabolism. Fasting triggers the production of HGH. It not only regulates your metabolism but it promotes the development of muscles and bones and balances your body composition. Production of HGH typically reduces with age. Nevertheless, all this can be reversed by fasting.

In parallel, another important cellular change that occurs is the production of noradrenaline. This hormone is important in regulating your body's ability to burn fats. Since fats are the main source of energy during the absence of active food consumption, fat loss is one of the benefits of intermittent fasting. Coupled with noradrenaline production, this promotes weight loss and regulation in the long run.

As mentioned earlier, whenever you consume any food, only a portion is immediately used while the rest is stored in fat cells. Unless you stop eating, your body doesn't utilize these internal reserves of fats. Another cellular change that takes place is ketosis. Ketosis is not only natural but incredibly helpful, too. As you know, your body's primary source of energy is glucose whenever you consume food. Once all the glucose from the food you consume is used, your body actively starts looking for alternate energy sources. This is when the internal fat reserves are solicited. When your body dips into its internal reserves, fats are converted into energy molecules known as ketones, which quickly replace glucose as your primary source of energy. A wonderful thing about ketones is that ketone production isn't limited or reduced as long as there are sufficient reserves of fat present in the body. This stabilizes energy levels and keeps you going, even while fasting. Essentially, your body stays in ketosis as long as you don't consume any carbs or sugars. By increasing your intake of dietary fats and reducing the intake of unhealthy carbs and sugars, ketosis lasts for longer.

Myths about Intermittent Fasting

Intermittent fasting has become incredibly popular over recent years. Whenever something gains popularity, several misconceptions about it start circulating. In this section, we'll explore common myths about intermittent fasting and the corresponding facts. These myths can prevent you from attaining your weight loss and fitness goals, so being a little mindful is of the essence.

Myth #1: Small Meals Are Needed for Weight Loss

The most common myth about dietary protocols is that you need to consume small meals to promote and eventually trigger weight loss. If you're constantly eating, how can your body ever start burning fats? As mentioned, your body does not utilize its stored reserves unless you stop eating. Fasting reduces your insulin levels and promotes lipolysis, which is when your body starts burning its internal reserves of fats. If you constantly eat small meals, your body needs to expend a significant portion of its energy digesting the food you are consuming. Also, this increases blood sugar levels. All in all, small meals do not or rarely aid weight loss. If you want to lose weight and burn fats, you need to fast.

It's important to realize that your calorie intake will not magically be reduced with small meals. For instance, if you need to consume 2000 calories daily, you can eat three healthy and wholesome meals.

Whether they are three or six meals, the calorie intake doesn't change. Similarly, the energy expended by your body digesting these calories will also remain the same. Intermittent fasting promotes weight loss during its fasting window. During the eating window, you can schedule the meals according to your convenience, needs, goals, and more.

Myth #2: Skipping Breakfast is Harmful to Your Health

While following the intermittent fasting protocol, you can schedule it according to your usual lifestyle, habits, and daily requirements. If you are a breakfast eater, don't worry about skipping it. Similarly, if you don't like the idea of having breakfast, don't eat it. This should be the only consideration. Don't be under the misconception that skipping breakfast is necessarily harmful to one's health. In fact, if you think about it for a moment, the key to weight loss is reducing your calorie intake. There is no scientific evidence to support the claim that skipping breakfast can promote weight gain. So, you can stop worrying about weight gain whenever you skip breakfast. While fasting it is most important to schedule the meals so that they help satiate your appetite.

Myth #3: Intermittent Fasting Increases Nutritional Deficiencies

Intermittent fasting encourages you to fast daily. That said, it doesn't mean you are not eating food altogether. Instead, the eating window is restricted. Nutritional deficiencies occur when you don't pay attention to the type of foods you are consuming. By increasing your intake of wholesome and nutrient-dense ingredients, the chances of nutritional deficiencies are reduced. This is one reason you need to pay a lot of attention to the food choices you make, something most of us have complete control over. Go through the list of ingredients and food choices discussed in the next sections and the meal plan provided in this book to ensure your body gets all the nutrients it needs. If you are worried about any nutritional deficiencies, discuss them with your physician or healthcare provider. If needed, you can always opt for a nutrient supplement.

Myth #4: Intermittent Fasting Causes Eating Disorders

Intermittent fasting does not cause eating disorders. This is nothing more than a myth. If you eat a healthy diet and follow the fasting protocols to the letter, the chances of developing an eating disorder are almost non-existent. However, if you have a history of eating disorders (for example bulimia or anorexia) or are recovering from one, do not attempt fasting unless you have made a full recovery. Eating disorders arise when you go overboard and severely restrict your food intake. Rather than expose yourself to potentially harmful risks, eat until your body is full and always opt for healthy and wholesome ingredients.

Myth #5: Intermittent Fasting Can Cause Infertility

It's a popular misconception that fasting causes infertility in women. The hormonal changes in women's bodies are quite real, yet they don't result in any fertility issues. That said, if you are nursing, trying to conceive, or pregnant, fasting (or any other diet, for that matter) is not recommended. A woman's body is highly sensitive to signs of starvation. If your food intake is drastically reduced, your body may misinterpret it as starvation. Starvation can trigger hormonal imbalances. So, once again, it is important to pay attention to the food you are consuming and its quality.

Myth #6: Intermittent Fasting Can Result in Muscle Loss

People believe fasting results in muscle loss. As long as your body has internal reserves of energy to sustain itself and you consume healthy and wholesome meals during the eating window, you don't have to worry about muscle loss. Your body doesn't use muscle protein unless it has run out of all possible energy sources. So, starving is not a good idea. Intermittent fasting promotes weight loss without reducing your muscle mass. In fact, you can even increase your muscle mass by combining the protocol of intermittent fasting with a healthy diet and a good exercise routine.

Myth #7: Overeating Is a Common Side Effect of Intermittent Fasting

Regulating your appetite and making healthy dietary choices are two fundamental aspects of this diet that are well within your control. Overeating doesn't occur if you fill up on nutrient-dense and fiber-rich foods. During the first few days, your body is getting accustomed to intermittent fasting, and the chances of slightly overeating may increase. Once your body is used to fasting, this does not happen or rarely does. To reduce the risk of overeating, make sure you have intermittent fasting-friendly meals and snacks on hand. When delicious and nutritious meals are waiting for you, it becomes easier to eat healthily. Also, this reduces the urge to binge on sweet snacks and unhealthy junk food. Remind yourself that fasting doesn't have to be difficult—by changing your mindset about fasting and giving your diet a little conscious consideration, fasting becomes easy. You will learn more about doing all this in the subsequent chapters.

Myth #8: The Brain Needs a Constant Supply of Dietary Groups

People believe that abstaining from eating carbs every couple of hours will reduce their cognitive functioning. This is primarily based on the belief that your brain requires only glucose to support itself. In reality, the human body is quite resourceful and capable of adjusting and adapting to existing conditions. If you are not constantly eating carbs, your body produces glucose through a process known as gluconeogenesis. Even during a prolonged fast, your body produces sufficient ketones from its internal fat reserves. These ketones can fuel your brain and fulfill its glucose requirements. That said, if you feel lightheadedness or extreme fatigue after fasting, chances are you are not eating properly. It may also be a sign that your eating-fasting window schedule isn't suited to your needs and lifestyle.

In the end, you must let go of any misconceptions about intermittent fasting before you follow its protocols. Whether it is for your health or weight loss goals, intermittent fasting is incredibly effective when done right.

Chapter 3: The Benefits of Fasting

Intermittent fasting is growing popular these days, and for all the right reasons. Whether you want to lose weight and maintain weight loss or improve your overall health, intermittent fasting is a wonderful and accessible option. In this section, we'll look at all the various benefits of fasting.

Regulates Blood Sugar Levels

Whenever you consume any food, the pancreas secretes a hormone known as insulin. Insulin is essential in converting this food into glucose, an easily absorbable source of energy. Glucose is then transported to different cells across the body. Insulin is responsible for regulating your blood sugar levels. Type-2 diabetes has become a pandemic these days. It is a condition whereby your body is incapable of producing the insulin required to stabilize blood sugar levels (also known as insulin resistance). It occurs when your body starts developing immunity toward natural insulin secretion. Even though the pancreas does produce insulin, it is not the desired level to manage and balance blood sugar levels.

According to a study conducted by Terra G. Arnason et al. (2017), intermittent fasting can reduce blood sugar levels in individuals with type-2 diabetes. According to a review undertaken by Adrienne R. Barnosky et al. (2014), intermittent fasting reduces insulin resistance due to the automatic calorie reduction it engenders. So, even though you are not counting calories while following this diet, the benefits it offers don't go away.

By curbing insulin resistance, your body's sensitivity to insulin increases. This makes it easier for the glucose to circulate in the bloodstream and enter the cells more efficiently. This beneficial effect, combined with its blood sugar-reducing reaction, can help stabilize your blood sugar levels. As such, the risk of any spikes or crashes in blood sugar levels is significantly reduced. If you have type-2 diabetes it is recommended you seek medical advice before attempting intermittent fasting.

Tackles Inflammation

Your body's primary line of defense against the presence of any disease-causing pathogens or foreign bodies is inflammation. In limited amounts, inflammation is crucial for your overall health and wellbeing; it is a natural immune response. Usually, once the threat is neutralized, inflammation subsides. Unfortunately, when inflammation persists, it can manifest into a chronic health problem. In chronic inflammation, the immune system mistakenly attacks itself and other healthy cells, causing internal damage. It is also believed to be the precursor for several severe health conditions, including heart disease, rheumatoid arthritis, and even certain cancers.

According to the results obtained by a study conducted by Mo'ez Al-Islam E Faris et al. (2012), fasting regularly for an entire month can reduce inflammatory markers. These claims are also backed by another study conducted by Fehime B Aksungar et al. (2007). In an animal study conducted by In-Young Choi et al. (2016), any diet that mimics the eating patterns prescribed by fasting reduces inflammation. The researchers of this study believe this can help treat inflammatory conditions such as multiple sclerosis.

Stabilizes Blood Pressure and Cholesterol Levels

According to the 2017 report presented by The American Heart Association, heart disease accounted for around 31% of deaths globally, quite a startling and disturbing figure. The two common health markers associated with an increase in cardiovascular disorders are high cholesterol levels and high blood pressure. Shifting to intermittent fasting is a good idea to improve your heart health. According to a study conducted by Surabhi Bhutani et al. (2010), following intermittent fasting reduces blood triglycerides by 32% and cholesterol levels by 25%, all within eight weeks. In another study conducted on 110 obese adults by Biljana Beleslin et al. (2007), intermittent fasting seemed to reduce their levels of blood pressure, cholesterol, and triglycerides. By improving the primary markers associated with coronary disease, fasting can greatly improve your cardiovascular health.

Improves Cognitive Functioning

It turns out that ancient Greeks were onto something when they believed fasting could promote cognitive functioning. Remember the "food coma" discussed in the previous chapters? In truth, fasting has a powerful effect on brain health. According to Li Liao et al. (2013), fasting can improve the brain's structure and function. Though most of the research available in this aspect is from animal models, fasting seems to offer promising potential in improving brain health. In another study conducted by J. Lee et al. (2000), fasting promoted new neural cells in mice. Similarly, the results from a study by M. Tajes et al. (2010) indicated that intermittent fasting helped enhance cognitive functioning.

Promotes Weight Loss

One of the most compelling reasons why people turn to intermittent fasting is its great potential for weight loss. The primary concept of weight loss is the need for a calorie deficit. A calorie deficit occurs when your calorie intake is lower than calorie expenditure (in other words, you "burn" more than you eat). According to G. Zauner et al. (2000), short-term fasting increases the production of norepinephrine, a neurotransmitter believed to trigger weight loss by activating your body's internal fat-burning mechanism. According to a review by Grant M. Tinsley et al. (2015), intermittent fasting for 12-24 weeks could result in a significant decline in body fat and weight.

Another benefit of following intermittent fasting is it naturally promotes calorie restriction. The fact that your meal timings are restricted means the chances of mindlessly binging on foods are reduced. It also makes you more conscious of your body's hunger and satiety cues. A combination of these factors can help reduce your calorie consumption, provided you make healthy choices. Considering this approach, intermittent fasting is the ideal dieting protocol for weight loss and maintenance.

Stimulates Metabolism

Several hormones are secreted by your body to maintain your overall health and function. One hormone is the human growth hormone, or HGH. The production of this hormone naturally declines with age. Unfortunately, an HGH deficiency can have severe effects on your health.

According to research by A Juul et al. (1995), intermittent fasting promotes the production of growth hormones. HGH is essential for maintaining muscle strength, stamina, body temperature, kidney function, and weight management. According to a study conducted by N. Moller et al. (1991), it improves glucose metabolism in the body. In another study by Michael Hojby Rasmussen (2010), it was shown that a reduction in the production of HGH increases the risk of obesity. The simplest way to reverse it is by increasing the production of HGH.

According to a study conducted by B. Salgin et al. (2012), it was noticed that fasting for even 12 hours causes a significant increase in HGH production. These claims are supported by the findings of a study by M. L. Hartman et al. (1992), which suggests fasting increases HGH secretion. The levels of HGH can be further optimized when blood sugar and insulin levels are stabilized. Since intermittent fasting helps achieve this objective, it further increases the production of HGH.

Reduces the Risk of Cancer

According to animal and test-tube studies, intermittent fasting may also help prevent and improve the efficiency of treatments in tackling cancer. According to a study by Noeme Sousa Rocha et al. (2002), intermittent fasting can block the formation of tumors in rats. In another test-tube study conducted by Changhan Lee et al. (2013), intermittent fasting was shown to delay the growth of tumors. Lee and his research team noticed that regular fasting had a similar effect on cancerous cells as in chemotherapy. Their findings also suggest that intermittent fasting can improve the efficiency of chemotherapy drugs used to tackle cancer formation.

Although these results and findings are derived from animal studies, the potential offered by intermittent fasting cannot be disregarded. Despite these promising results, extensive research is still needed to fully understand how intermittent fasting can reduce the risks associated with cancer.

Kick-Starts Autophagy

As mentioned earlier, autophagy is a cellular change that occurs while fasting. This term refers to your body's internal mechanism responsible for cellular repair. In autophagy, the damaged cells are actively cannibalized by the healthy cells. Once the undesirable cells are all eliminated, it leaves room for more healthy and helpful cells to be produced. Self-cannibalization might sound worrisome, but it has a wonderful benefit. Over time, certain cells are damaged and may even cease to function altogether. These cells must be removed so your body can function optimally and create healthier cells again. This is where autophagy plays its role.

Easily Sustainable

Apart from all the different benefits mentioned so far, another advantage of intermittent fasting that cannot be overlooked is the convenience it offers. The 16/8 protocol is incredibly simple to follow and can be customized according to your needs and requirements. You can shift the fasting and eating windows according to your convenience, making it perfectly sustainable in the long run. Unlike most conventional diets, intermittent fasting doesn't place any restrictions on calorie counting or food restriction. Instead, it lets you eat to your heart's content, provided you don't consume any calories during the fasting window and opt for nutritional meals later.

Remember this: If you want to lose weight or improve your overall health, limit your intake of processed, prepackaged, and unhealthy foods. Rather than binge on unhealthy carbs and sugars and other foods devoid of nutrition, fill up on wholesome and nutritious meals during the eating window. You can do all this without worrying about the calories you consume.

When you combine all the advantages offered by the 16/8 protocol, it becomes evident why it has become so incredibly popular.

Chapter 4: What to Know before Fasting

After going through the various benefits of intermittent fasting, chances are you are quite excited about getting started. This customizable and sustainable diet is ideal for all healthy adults, but everything has its limitations. This section will look at a few important considerations you need to keep in mind before embarking on this diet.

Who Shouldn't Try Fasting?

If you fall into any of the categories mentioned in the section, refrain from fasting.

Fasting is neither ideal nor encouraged for pregnant women. The nutritional requirements of a pregnant woman differ from the needs of others. Your body not only has to sustain itself but support the fetus as well. While fasting is safe for most, attempting any form of diet during pregnancy is not recommended. To date, there is no scientific evidence to fully determine the effects of fasting on an unborn infant. That said, it is a common belief that fasting can disrupt your nutritional intake and, in turn, affect the nutritional needs of the fetus.

Aside from pregnant women, if you are breastfeeding, you should not attempt fasting or any diet for that matter. Once again, your body's requirements at this time are quite different, and right now, your primary focus should only be on taking care of yourself and the baby. Fasting can wait a few months. A woman's body is quite sensitive to signals of starvation. Even if fasting is a voluntary choice, your body cannot distinguish between starvation and a voluntary fast. Whenever this happens, your body's primary focus shifts to its survival. This survival instinct prevents all other non-essential functions in favor of survival, such as reproduction. If you are trying to conceive, avoid fasting or making any drastic changes to your regular diet.

If you have any preexisting health conditions, or liver or kidney troubles, fasting is not advised. If you suffer from bouts of weakness, are malnourished, or anemic, fasting is not recommended at all. Before you start fasting, consider seeing your healthcare provider for their medical opinion. Similarly, certain medications should never be taken while fasting. If you use medicines to regulate your blood pressure, treat a weak immune system or due to poor blood circulation, avoid fasting altogether. If you want to try your hand at fasting, make sure to consult your healthcare provider beforehand.

If you are recovering from an eating disorder or have a history of eating disorders, attempting any diet, even intermittent fasting, is not advisable. Whether it is bulimia or anorexia or any other eating disorder, your body needs a while to recover from the condition. So, unless you are 100% recovered and your doctor has cleared you for fasting, don't try it.

If you are recovering from an illness, have recently undergone major surgery, or are preparing for major surgery, avoid fasting. Following a diet that restricts the eating window during these periods is not recommended. Your primary nutritional requirements differ during the recovery period, and fasting can harm this process. You can start fasting once you have fully recovered. Once again, do not forget to consult your physician or dietitian before attempting this diet.

Fasting is not encouraged for children. Occasional fasting for short periods will not harm them, yet a long-term fasting protocol is far from ideal. A child's body requires plenty of nutrition to grow healthily and sustain itself. Your child's pediatrician must approve the diet before you make any drastic changes to it. According to certain laws and provisions in the United States, it is illegal for a child to fast. By contrast, obese children are allowed to fast under adult supervision and a doctor's guidance in Europe, provided the child does so voluntarily.

All healthy adults can fast without any major worries. Fasting regularly cleanses your system from the inside, and there are no reasons why a healthy adult should abstain from fasting. Among several benefits already listed, fasting regulates the levels of blood sugar.

Remember, before making any dietary changes, don't forget to consult your healthcare provider.

Considerations before Fasting

The 16/8 protocol is incredibly simple and doesn't require any drastic lifestyle changes. Apart from your state of health, there are three simple considerations you need to remember before starting this diet. The first consideration is your personal opinion about fasting. The second one is your daily schedule, and the third, your regular diet. These three factors may sound unimportant, but they are in fact crucial for determining your motivation while following intermittent fasting.

While making dietary changes may sound simple, a significant change in your body and mind is required. Unless you have an open mind about fasting, starting intermittent fasting can be tricky. Remember, you need to restrict the eating window to only eight hours daily. This means you need to fast for sixteen hours. Unless you are mentally prepared for the diet, making this change will prove extremely difficult. Your personal opinion about fasting also determines your level of investment in the diet. Ensure that you are comfortable with the idea of fasting and that it does not become a source of additional stress. We already lead busy and hectic lifestyles, and diet must not be a source of added stress or a burden. Take time and carefully consider how this protocol works. Unless you are completely comfortable with the idea of fasting, do not attempt it. If doubts persist, you are only increasing the chances of giving up on this diet. This may, in turn, demotivate you from attempting to fast in the future. If you want to fast and are genuinely interested, keep an open mind and work on changing your mindset.

Evidently, your regular diet plays a significant role in your life. Take time and carefully consider what your usual diet looks like. If it is predominantly made up of processed foods, carbs, sugars, and other prepackaged foods, shifting to this new diet will take a good deal of time. Believe it or not, a diet rich in carbs and sugar is rather addictive. Your mindset aside, you need to gradually condition your body to the idea of depriving it of food temporarily. If you've never fasted before and this is your first attempt, take a little extra time.

While shifting to this diet is simple, you need to be patient. For instance, if you are used to constantly snacking or consuming high-calorie foods, slowly increase the amount of time between two meals and reduce the number of snacks you consume. Another simple suggestion to make the transition easier is to replace carbs and processed foods with nutrient-dense and wholesome ingredients.

The third consideration is your usual schedule or lifestyle. Intermittent fasting is not complicated and offers great flexibility, unlike other dietary protocols. That said, you cannot follow a diet if it clashes with or somehow impedes your regular schedule. For instance, if you are in the habit of skipping breakfast, following this protocol becomes all the more simple. Similarly, if you like the idea of waking up early in the morning and getting in a good workout, shift the eating window accordingly. Regardless of your daily lifestyle, intermittent fasting can be customized with a little conscious thought and planning.

You must spend time carefully thinking about all these considerations; after all, your chances of sticking to this diet depend on them.

Chapter 5: Understanding Weight Loss Differences between Men and Women

A factor commonly blamed for weight gain is a slow metabolism. Chances are, you've heard this phrase tossed around in casual conversations. What does "metabolism" really mean, and what role does it play in weight loss? Let us answer these two questions in this chapter to explain the difference between weight loss in men and women.

Understanding Body Metabolism

Several processes are constantly working behind the scenes in your body. From respiration to digestion, hormone regulation, growth and repair of cells, and blood circulation, every system in your body requires energy to function efficiently. These functions tend to go on in the background even when you are resting. In reality, none of these processes ever stop. Most of these involuntary functions are crucial for your wellbeing and health. So, where does this energy come from? Simply put, the metabolism is the primary process that enables your body to transform the food you consume into energy.

During metabolism, the calories in the food you consume mingle with oxygen in the bloodstream and are transformed into the energy your body needs to function.

This process is known as metabolism or basal metabolic rate. Different factors determine your basal metabolic rate. The most common factors to pay attention to are sex, age, body size, and composition. Those with more developed muscles or a larger body tend to have more calories they can burn even while resting. Calorie burning is reduced as you age because the amount of muscle present in the body tends to diminish while fat increases. Sex also plays a significant role when it comes to your body's metabolism. From a biological point of view, men tend to have more muscle and less fat than women of the same age and weight. This is one of the reasons why men tend to burn more calories than women.

Beyond all these factors, your body's main functions and the energy it needs is fairly constant. Two additional factors determine the calories you burn daily, namely thermogenesis and physical activity. As mentioned earlier, the food you eat is transformed into energy by your body. Whenever you eat, the food is first digested, then absorbed, transported, and a portion of it is stored before it is assimilated and expelled. This entire process is known as thermogenesis.

Simply put, it is nothing more than food processing. Only about 10% of the calories obtained from the proteins and carbs you consume are used during digestion and food absorption. Physical activity in all its forms and exercise account for the number of calories your body burns daily.

Now that you understand what metabolism is and the factors that influence it, let's explore the relationship between metabolism and weight. A fairly common assumption is that your metabolism is to blame for weight gain. Since metabolism is a natural and essential process for survival, several mechanisms are in place to regulate it and ensure all its needs are fulfilled. Excessive weight gain due to a metabolic problem is not common; this usually occurs when the thyroid gland is underactive or subject to conditions such as Cushing's syndrome. Weight gain is not as simple as this. Instead, it is a severely complicated process. It is the culmination of genetic and hormonal makeup and composition, diet, as well as your daily lifestyle and environment. Should there be an imbalance in any of these factors, it will cause an imbalance in the whole system; for instance, if you eat more calories than your body burns, the result will be weight gain.

It is true some people can lose weight more quickly than others. If you want to lose weight, you must make sure your body burns more calories than you consume. No one is exempt from this rule. By devising a diet that causes an energy deficit or increases the calories burned during the day, you can lose weight.

You might not have much control over how quickly the basal metabolic rate works, but you can regulate the number of calories burned through physical activity. The more physically active you are, the greater the calories burned. This is one reason why fasting increases your body's metabolism by promoting the calories burned during the fasting period. The simplest and most efficient way to burn calories is through aerobic ("cardio") activities such as jogging, walking, cycling, or yoga. Even engaging in thirty minutes of physical activity daily can significantly increase your calorie expenditure.

If you have specific fitness or weight loss goals, the level of physical activity required may be higher. If you cannot exercise for half-an-hour, you can break it down into ten-minute intervals and include them into your daily routine. Besides aerobic activities, strength training exercises such as weightlifting, help to build your muscles while reducing the fatty tissues present within. What does all this mean? Essentially, that all the extra movement increases calorie expenditure.

Weight Loss in Men and Women

You might have heard that men are from Mars while women are from Venus. This popular book on relationships explains the differences between how men and women communicate, express their emotions, and behave in general. There is another aspect of life where women and men differ: how the metabolism works for weight loss.

Previously, women were primarily interested in losing weight and maintaining a thin physique due to social or cultural pressure more than health concerns (at least in Western societies). Men were primarily focused on building muscles, taking supplements, and enhancing their muscles. Nowadays, a shift has occurred in what men and women are trying to achieve. Both genders are now more focused on reducing fat while maintaining a leaner physique. However, there are a couple of differences between the sexes due to our genetic coding. This section will look at all the different factors that result in varying weight loss for men and women.

From a strictly genetic standpoint, men have more muscle mass and less fat than women. This difference is due to higher levels of testosterone in men. This is why their calorie consumption is typically higher than women's to maintain muscle mass and body weight. Suppose you compare two individuals with similar body weight, but one has more muscle mass than the other. In that case, the person with greater muscle mass requires more calories to sustain their weight because their calorie expenditure is higher. Muscle tends to burn more calories than fat does, even at rest. A general notion is that around 3500 calories are required for one pound of muscle mass. Whenever you are trying to lose weight, only about half of the weight loss is from muscles. By concentrating on what you eat and including strength training, you can considerably minimize muscle loss. Usually, both men and women start losing muscle mass during their thirties. In parallel, loss of muscle also affects the immune system and mobility.

How we carry our body weight is also quite different based on which gender we are. If men gain a little weight, the primary area where it goes is the abdomen. This explains why most men are "apple-shaped." On the other hand, premenopausal women tend to put on weight near the hips and less in the abdominal region. Due to hormonal changes during menopause, post-menopausal women usually gain weight in the abdominal region because of a reduction in estrogen.

Regardless of gender, any excess fat that starts accumulating in the abdominal area and around the organs bears significant health risks. This is known as visceral fat, which is highly inflammatory. This unhealthy fat is directly associated with an increased risk of cardiovascular disorders, fatty liver disease, and diabetes. In contrast, the soft fat present directly under the skin isn't metabolically dangerous and is responsible for regulating your body temperature and overall state of health.

This brings us to another important notion about weight loss, which states that men can lose weight more easily than women. A popular theory is associated with the role of hormones and the brain's response to calorie restriction. From an evolutionary point of view, a woman's body is genetically designed for reproduction. This activity requires significant energy. Whenever the brain notices a reduction in energy available, it tends to divert all the available resources for life-sustaining activities, and reproduction is not one of them. This is one reason why excessive calorie restriction in women causes irregularities in menstrual cycles and might also lead to fertility issues. All in all, a woman's body needs a greater percentage of body fat when compared to a man.

These differences in body fat percentage are all a part of our basic physiology. Men tend to have a weight-loss edge over women due to their elevated testosterone levels and low levels of estrogen.

On average, women tend to have anywhere between 6-11% more body fat than men. From puberty to menopause, even when women consume fewer calories than men, their average body fat level is higher. Now, it is important to understand that fat isn't always synonymous with unhealthiness. Even if women have larger fat stores, this does not necessarily mean extra weight. If a woman has 10% more body fat than a man, it doesn't mean she is 10% "fatter." A perfectly fit and healthy woman will have 6-11% more body fat than a healthy man.

This basic difference in physiology, coupled with how fats are stored in the body, results in differences in weight loss. As mentioned earlier, fats in men accumulate in the abdominal region while fats tend to be more spread out in women. So, the weight loss is more noticeable and visible in men than women because of how the internal reserves of fats are stored. Despite differences in weight loss between men and women, these tend to even out in the long run. Even if women are better at storing fats, their body's ability to burn more fat during exercise is higher than men.

In the end, weight loss is an achievable and maintainable goal for adult men and women alike. Forget about your gender, and instead shift your attention toward leading a healthier life, exercising regularly, and consuming a healthy diet. Once you do all this, weight loss and maintenance become easy, regardless of whether you are a woman or a man.

Chapter 6: How to Exercise While Fasting

Intermittent fasting and regular exercise are the simplest ways to improve your overall health while attaining fitness and weight loss goals. When it comes to weight loss and muscle gain, calories are not the only factors that play an important role; exercise also helps hormone optimization. By combining these two aspects, attaining your fitness and health goals becomes easier and more manageable. A combination of exercise and diet aids the production of growth hormones and increases insulin sensitivity.

It is rather unfortunate that most people obsess over the calories they consume and spend. Some are also worried about muscle loss. Muscle loss occurs only when you exercise without refueling your body. By understanding the positive effects of exercise on the hormones in your body during the fasting state, you'll realize that fasting improves muscle health and promotes fat loss at the same time.

If you are worried about exercising on an empty stomach, it's time to put these fears to rest! It is not only okay to exercise on an empty stomach, but it increases the benefits of exercise as well. Intermittent fasting is simply an extension of the period your body goes without food, including the time you sleep. The fasting window stretches the last bite of food you consumed, until you eat again. As such, the ideal time to work out is after you wake up in the morning. This works with your body's internal circadian rhythm (which regulates sleep) and boosts the benefits of working out.

Exercise Options

If you are eager to add exercise into your daily routine, here are the best, true and tested options to go for.

Cardio

Cardio is a form of aerobic activity that engages different muscle groups in your body. Whether it is walking, running, jogging, biking or swimming, these are all examples of aerobic activities. The hormonal benefits of exercising during a fasted state are associated with depletion of glycogen stored in the muscles and liver. You can indulge in cardio while fasting, but your overall performance throughout depends on your body's stage of fat adaptation. Fat adaptation refers to a state whereby your body no longer depends on glycogen to support itself and instead concentrates on burning the internal reserves of fat to fuel its energy requirements.

Invariably, it will take your body some time to get used to the new diet. During the initial days, you may notice a dip in your usual performance. Once your body is used to burning fats, your performance is bound to improve. If you are exercising in a fasted state, don't forget to refuel after the exercise. Otherwise, it increases the risk of starvation. Finally, it is very important to note that if your body shifts to a state of starvation, it stops burning fats and instead hoards all calories to sustain itself.

Sprint Training

High-intensity interval training (HIIT), also known as sprint training, involves short bursts of exercise followed by a period of rest or recovery. A typical HIIT workout lasts anywhere between

15-30 minutes. This form of exercise is time-efficient and offers health benefits that surpass those of traditional aerobic exercises. HIIT can increase your strength, stamina, promote cognitive function, increase growth hormones, and improve your body composition. Sprint training can be easily incorporated into your intermittent fasting schedule. To maximize the benefits of this exercise, make sure that you stay in the fasted state for at least two hours after exercising.

Lifting Weights

Lifting weights helps develop and strengthen the muscles, increase stamina, and build lean body fat. Lifting weights in a fasted state is fine. However, you need to pay a little attention to the role of glucose. After lifting weights, your muscles need additional glucose to repair and restore themselves. In a fasted state, your body first depletes the available reserves of glycogen (stored glucose) before moving on to burning fats. If your workout includes lifting weights, you can do so even in a fasted state, but you need to refuel your body once the workout is over. Unlike sprint training, lifting weights increases the stress on your body. As with cardio, you will need a while to increase your body's ability to power through a full weightlifting session. You may notice a decline in your endurance during the phase of adaptation; once your body turns on its internal fat-burning mechanism, exercising becomes easier. So, if you want to lift weights, make sure that you do so after eating.

Exercise Tips

Before you start exercising on the 16/8 protocol, bear in mind the following.

The first thing you need to consider is the timing of the exercise. If you've never attempted fasting before, it will be a significant change for your body to adapt to. To facilitate the transition and improve the workout's efficiency while fasting, you need to decide when you want to exercise. You can exercise before, after, or during the eating window.

The 16/8 protocol is one of the most popular methods of intermittent fasting. Suppose you believe your overall performance while exercising is superior on an empty stomach. In that case, you can exercise before the eating window. If you don't like the idea of exercising on an empty stomach, then do it during the eating window. The same rule applies to anyone who wants to capitalize on nutrition after working out. Performance and recovery are usually optimized after your body has sufficient fuel available. For instance, if you are lifting weights or performing cardio, you must refuel your body afterward. For these exercises, the ideal time is to exercise on an empty stomach right before the fasting window ends. This allows you to refuel your body, promote muscle development and stimulate fat loss.

Another important consideration to remember is the type of workout you opt for according to your macronutrient intake. Pay attention to the macros you consume in a day before you exercise, and anytime you eat later is important. For instance, cardio or high-intensity interval training can be performed even if your carbohydrate intake is low. By contrast, you need a significantly higher amount of carbs in your system to power through a strength training session.

To build and maintain muscle mass, it's not just important to exercise—you need to pay attention to the diet, too. If this is your main motivation for exercising, you need to make sure you consume food immediately after working out. One of the major advantages of combining intermittent fasting and exercise is that you get a chance to time the workout during the eating window, so your body gets all the nutrients it needs. Once again, you need to consume carbs and proteins in sufficient amounts after heavy lifting to promote muscle regeneration and muscle development. If you are indulging in any strength training, you need to consume around 20 grams of carbs and proteins within one hour of exercising.

Now that you're aware of all these dietary considerations, here are a few tips you can use to promote the efficiency of your exercise regimen and weight loss.

As established, meal timing is crucial when it comes to exercising. During high-intensity or moderate-intensity workouts, you need to eat something close to the workout schedule. This ensures your body has sufficient glycogen to power through the workout. For these exercises, the ideal time is after the eating window ends.

It isn't just food that matters when it comes to exercise. In fact, you need to ensure thorough hydration. Fasting doesn't mean you don't drink any water; if you are dehydrated, it increases stress on the muscles and reduces your workout efficiency. It also increases the risk of burning out. In parallel, you must also maintain your electrolyte levels. A good source of hydration helps replenish your electrolytes and is low in calories. That said, drinking Gatorade, Powerade, or any other sports drink loaded with sugars during the fasting window is not recommended.

During the initial days of shifting to intermittent fasting, your energy levels will fluctuate. In this transition period, you need to be extremely patient; there's no point in rushing into high-intensity training when your energy levels are low or wavering. Once your body is accustomed to the new fasting schedule, your energy levels will stabilize, making it easier to work out efficiently. During the initial period, any form of gentle exercises such as walking, yoga, Pilates, and jogging will suffice. Take it at your pace.

Last but definitely not least, one thing you should never forget is to listen to your own body's cues. The human body is quite smart, and it knows what it needs. If you feel weak or dizzy, it can be a sign of dehydration or low blood sugar levels. If so, stop exercising and have a carbohydrate and electrolyte mix immediately. If you are too tired to exercise, pay attention to your body's needs and requirements. Unless you take good care of it, it cannot function, much less actively or efficiently. Before you start any exercise regimen, don't forget to consult your healthcare provider or a professional trainer. This is especially true if you have any preexisting health conditions that can affect your mobility.

Chapter 7: Beginning the 16/8 Fasting Diet

Congratulations on making it this far! By now, you are aware of the various benefits intermittent fasting offers. Shifting to this diet immediately might be tempting, but a little planning and preparation are needed before you make any changes. In this insightful chapter, you will be introduced to simple dietary suggestions and steps you can follow to get started on the 16/8 diet.

What to Eat During the Fasting Window

The only rule to remember during the fasting window is that you should not consume any calories. If you consume calories, your body shifts from a fast to a fed state. That said, it doesn't mean you cannot drink any calorie-free beverages. In this section, let's look at a couple of options you can safely consume during the fasting window.

Apple Cider Vinegar

One of the best things you can consume during the fasting window without any worries is apple cider vinegar. Apple cider vinegar helps stabilize the electrolyte levels, reduces hunger pangs and rebalances pH levels in the digestive tract. Apple cider vinegar is known to have anti-inflammatory and antibacterial properties that help strengthen your immune system and promote proper digestive functioning. Moreover, it gives your metabolism a quick boost, which is much needed for burning fats efficiently. Apple cider vinegar also contains essential minerals such as potassium, magnesium, and iron, all good for your health.

Baking Soda

While it is commonly used in cooking, you may be surprised to learn that you can drink baking soda! Your body's internal pH tends to change during the fasting period. Drinking a little baking soda helps restore this pH balance. It also alleviates tiredness, making you feel more energetic. Add a teaspoon of food-grade baking soda to a glass of water and drink it during the fasting period to keep hunger pangs or cravings at bay. Sodium bicarbonate or baking soda replenishes any lost sodium during the fasting period. As mentioned, ketosis can have a diuretic effect, which means your body starts to lose its internal reserves of sodium and water. Baking soda helps neutralize this while keeping you hydrated.

Herbal Teas

Sipping on herbal teas is an efficient and delicious way to tackle hunger pangs during the fasting period. Simply make sure that you do not add any sugar, sweeteners, or honey to your cup of herbal tea. A freshly brewed cup of peppermint tea can re-energize and refresh your mind, whereas chamomile tea has a calming and soothing effect. Depending on what you are in the mood for, sip on a cup of freshly brewed herbal tea to feel better. You can also drink unsweetened green tea; it is rich in antioxidants that tackle inflammation and promote your body's metabolism to burn fats efficiently.

Glauber's Salt

Taking Glauber's salt or sodium sulfate decahydrate is an excellent way to boost your metabolism while making it easier to get through the fasting period. It also helps to stabilize your electrolyte levels and prevent dehydration. Glauber's salt is safe for daily consumption. That said, do not consume more than 20 grams of salts on any given day. Add a teaspoon of the salt to a glass of water and drink it whenever you are fasting. These salts act as mild laxatives and improve digestion while relieving uncomfortable symptoms of constipation. So, consuming too much of these salts can result in diarrhea.

Coffee

Coffee is a great way to suppress hunger while fasting. It not only gives you an instant boost of energy but also helps to stabilize your blood sugar levels and promote fat utilization. If the eating window starts at noon, you can start your day with a cup of black coffee. Once again, you mustn't add any milk, creamer, sugar, or any other sweetener to your cup of coffee. You can, however, add a pinch of cinnamon or cocoa powder to give your morning coffee a more interesting profile. Remember, coffee is a natural diuretic, and consuming too much of it can quickly dehydrate you. Excess caffeine can trigger anxiety, increase stress, and disrupt your sleeping pattern. Avoid consuming coffee past 8 p.m. in the evening. In parallel, make sure you drink sufficient water to keep your body hydrated and well-lubricated.

Consuming these calorie-free beverages during your fasting period makes it easier to stamp out any hunger pangs. Most of these healthy options assist the beneficial cellular changes triggered by fasting.

How to Break a Fast

As mentioned in the previous chapter, you need to slowly get your body accustomed to fasting for prolonged periods following the 16/8 protocol. Since you will be fasting daily, how you break your fast is of utmost importance.

Fasting may sound simple, especially in the initial stages when your motivation is quite high. Unless you plan for it, following this diet will become tricky in the long run. Reduce the chances of giving up on this diet by letting go of an "I can wing it" mentality. You need a proper plan of action if you want to improve your overall health and fitness levels. "Failing to plan is planning to fail"— remember this mantra in all aspects of your life!

As we've seen, several changes occur in your body during the fasting window. One of the most important changes is ketosis. The liver produces ketones to sustain you, which can increase the stress on your digestive system. So, breaking your fast properly is crucial in managing the stress on your digestive system. Excess stress can trigger inflammation and induce other complications. This further worsens when you consume unhealthy and processed foods rich in carbs and sugars. Inflammation is also a primary cause of weight gain. It also harms your immune system.

If you don't have a well-designed plan in place, chances are you will eat the first thing you can get your hands on after breaking the fast. You need to avoid certain foods, especially those rich in carbs, since this increases sodium retention. The chances of gaining weight spike when there is excess sodium present in the body. Remember, your body eliminates sodium during fasting. Binging on carbs reverses this process, triggering anti-diuresis that causes bloating. Apart from this, it can also reduce your energy levels.

Here is one reason you need to pay extra attention to how you end the fast. One of the best ways to end the fast is by consuming a little apple cider vinegar. It helps to restore the pH level in your gut, neutralizes harmful bacteria in the digestive tract, and regulates your blood sugar levels. Since it is a calorie-free ingredient, you can also consume it during the fasting period. However, the best time to have apple cider vinegar is as soon as you start the fast. If the taste of raw apple cider vinegar is off-putting, you can add a pinch of cinnamon and squeeze half a lime into a glass of water. To stabilize your electrolyte levels, don't hesitate to add a pinch of sea salt as well. Sip on this mixture for thirty minutes before breaking the fast. Alternatively, you can end the fast by drinking a glass of warm water mixed with a little honey and lemon juice. The citric acid stimulates the digestive enzymes and "warms up" your gut for the food you will eat after fasting.

Another healthy option is to drink a little bone broth. Bone broth is a superfood rich in electrolytes and essential nutrients your body needs. It also stimulates the production of digestive enzymes and facilitates the absorption of nutrients from the food you will consume later. While fasting, your body is in self-cleanse mode, and it needs a while to get used to digesting and absorbing food once you start eating. This is one reason you need to pay extra attention to what you eat after ending the fast. Likewise, you can drink vegetable broth, organic soups, or anything else easily digested. This simple habit reduces the chances of overeating or binging on unhealthy foods.

What to Eat Right after Breaking the Fast

Again, and this can never be stressed enough, it will take time to get used to fasting daily. Apart from preparing your body to break the fast, paying attention to what you eat after the fast ends is equally important. If you don't want to undo all the benefits of fasting, consuming a well-balanced diet is crucial.

If you end the fast by consuming foods rich in carbs and sodium, it increases water retention, which will result in weight gain. Since intermittent fasting's primary aim is weight loss, you must avoid foods that increase water retention. Your body needs to secrete insulin to transport the essential nutrients from one cell to another. A drastic spike in insulin levels, which occurs when you consume carbon sugars, can induce lethargy and drowsiness. So, make sure that the first meal you consume after breaking the fast has a low glycemic index. Meals like these help your body to stay in a semi-fasted state for longer and reduce blood sugar level fluctuations.

Don't worry about self-cannibalization of muscles if your body stays in ketosis for a while longer. This does not occur unless your body has thoroughly exhausted all the sources of energy at its disposal. If you follow the protocols of intermittent fasting properly, you will not shift into starvation mode. Eating a handful of nuts, eggs, spinach, and healthy fats, such as avocados, is an example of a low glycemic meal.

Another healthy option for ending your fast is eating fresh fruit. Fructose is the natural sugar present in fruit, which can be easily metabolized by the liver. This also helps replenish the depleted stores of glycogen. The liver can store anywhere between 100-150 grams of glycogen. While fasting, the glycogen reserves are exhausted before it starts burning fats. To replace the lost glycogen, eat fresh fruit. Fruit is also rich in nutrients and vitamins your body needs to function optimally. If you consume foods with a high glycemic index after breaking the fast, it will undo all your fasting efforts. Any foods rich in glycogen will increase fat accumulation. Ideally, opt for foods rich in fiber and low in sugar, such as berries, apples, and melons.

There are no dietary restrictions or calorie considerations you need to worry about while following the 16/8 protocol. However, this is no excuse to go overboard and binge on unhealthy foods. Since the eating window stretches over eight hours, you have ample time to consume all the calories your body needs. Ideally, the first meal should be no more than 500 calories. In reality, it becomes far easier to make sure your body gets all the nutrients it needs by planning your meals in advance. If you exercise before the fasting window ends, make sure you consume food that replenishes your glycogen stores.

The good news is, you don't have to spend hours on end searching for intermittent fasting-friendly recipes. All the recipes you need are provided in this book. Carefully go through them, select the ones that appeal to you, and create a meal plan accordingly. Once you have all the ingredients purchased and prepped, cooking becomes easier and more enjoyable. You'll be compelled to make healthier and more conscious food choices as well.

Basic Dietary Suggestions

In this section, we'll take a look at the different foods you can consume after your fast ends without worrying. All these options are rich in nutrients that your body needs and aid weight loss.

Leafy Vegetables

All leafy vegetables, including kale, spinach, Swiss chard, amaranth, and rosella, abound with antioxidants and various vitamins and minerals. They are also low in calories and rich in dietary fiber. Leafy greens are the perfect addition to any diet.

Fish

Fish is a phenomenal source of lean protein and heart-healthy Omega-3 fatty acids. Naturally fatty fish such as trout, sardines, salmon, mahi-mahi, and cod are superb options. You can consume anywhere between 5-8 ounces of fish daily without any worries. The Omega-3 fatty acids and other helpful nutrients found in fish can improve your cognitive functioning and cardiovascular health. Apart from that, they're quite easy on the digestive system, too. Whenever you choose to eat fish, opt for the ones caught in the wild instead of factory-farmed fish.

Legumes

Legumes are a great source of digestive fiber, vitamins, and nutrients that your body needs. All the digestive fiber present in legumes promotes digestion and better absorption of nutrients. Legumes are incredibly diverse, vegan-friendly, and a healthy source of carbohydrates. They can easily and safely be incorporated into any meal. The fiber found in legumes increases satiety without added calories, which is crucial in intermittent fasting; when your hunger is satiated, getting through the fasting window becomes easier.

Avocados

One of the best sources of healthy and natural dietary fats is avocado. Avocados are a superfood loaded with Omega 3 fatty acids and digestive fiber, and are a great source of health-boosting protein. From smoothies and whole wheat toasts to salads, avocados can be easily incorporated into your daily meals.

Probiotics

Did you know that your gut harbors millions of bacteria known as the "gut microbiome?" Don't worry, as not all types of bacteria are harmful. In fact, certain types of bacteria are desirable to promote digestion and absorption of nutrients. When the gut microbiome functions properly, your digestive health improves. It also reduces the risk of inflammation. The simplest way to feed the gut microbiome is by adding probiotics into your daily diet. Probiotics are live microorganisms that promote the health of the gut microbiome, and the most common types are fermented foods such as yogurt, kombucha, buttermilk, kimchi, and sauerkraut. Instead of the store-bought variants filled with additives, try to make these at home with simple ingredients.

Berries

There are countless types of berries to choose from, and they're all rich in vitamin A and C and several antioxidants. They are also low in calories. Different berries you can consume without any worries are raspberries, strawberries, blueberries, blackberries, and even cherries. You can add them to smoothies or even turn them into a guilt-free dessert. The antioxidants reverse oxidative stress, fight free radicals, and regulate inflammation. Berries are also believed to strengthen the immune system. Whether fresh or frozen, berries are bound to be a wonderful and tasty addition to your daily diet.

Whole Foods

Make it a point to consciously add healthier whole foods (brown bread, pasta, rice, etc.) to your diet instead of the processed variants. Whole foods are rich in dietary fibers and several nutrients good for overall health. They also improve your body's metabolism, digestive health, and help maintain satiety.

Healthy Carbs

Just because intermittent fasting doesn't impose strict dietary rules doesn't mean you should binge on unhealthy carbs. For instance, eating a bag of chips or a candy bar at the end of the fasting window does not do you any favors. Unhealthy carbs are rich in empty calories without any added nutrients. Instead, opt for low-carb fruits and vegetables.

Eggs

Eggs are a great source of protein and dietary fats. Consume at least two eggs daily to improve your health. They also have a low glycemic index and contain nutrients, so ending your fast by eating eggs is an accessible option. Eggs are low in calories, easy to cook, and very versatile.

Apart from all these foods, don't forget to drink sufficient water. You need to drink at least eight glasses (around two liters) of water daily. Water helps flush out any toxins present within the body in the dissolved fat. Whenever you make any dietary changes, hydration should be your priority. You can even add a sprig of fresh mint leaves or a couple of slices of lemon or cucumber to spruce up regular water and make it more interesting.

Getting Started with Intermittent Fasting

Now that you have all the information about intermittent fasting, it's time to get started. In this section, let's look at simple steps you can follow to successfully transition into the 16/8 intermittent fasting protocol.

Start with the Groundwork

The first step of shifting to intermittent fasting is to complete the required groundwork. Essentially, you need to carefully consider your usual schedule and lifestyle. Once you have a rough routine in place, determine the ideal timing for fasting. If you are used to waking up early in the morning and exercising, the fasting window will be quite different than for someone who prefers skipping breakfast. This first step is important because it determines whether the diet is sustainable in the long run. Carefully go through all the aspects covered until now, and it will become easy to determine how you wish to go about this diet.

Get the Tools Required

Don't be afraid to experiment with your diet. You can start with a specific fasting and eating routine and then shift to something else if you realize it isn't working. The process of trial and error is incredibly helpful when it comes to this protocol of intermittent fasting. In parallel, you will need plenty of recipes to design a meal plan that's ideal for intermittent fasting. All the recipes you need to create a detailed meal plan have been included in this book. Go through the recipes, put together a meal plan, and start batch cooking over the weekends to save time during the week.

While making a dietary change, pay special attention to what you are eating. The simplest way to do this is by keeping a food journal or using a mobile app to track what you eat. This is not the same as counting calories; the simple act of writing down your food choices makes you more conscious and allows you to make healthier choices in the future. This also helps you understand which foods work well with your metabolism.

Time to Transition

Shifting to intermittent fasting should not be a decision taken on a whim. If you want this diet to be sustainable, planning is needed. Take time, consider when you want to start this diet, and make a note of it. To transition into this diet, there are certain helpful changes you can make. For instance, if your usual diet is rich in carbs, slowly start cutting them down. If you are used to snacking constantly, stop snacking between meals and slowly increase the duration between two meals. By making these simple changes, controlling your hunger and shifting to intermittent fasting becomes easier. In a way, you are conditioning your body and mind to the idea of fasting daily. If you want, you can fast for brief periods daily to see how you feel about it and how your body responds.

Support System

Never underestimate the importance of having a support system in your life. Be it your friends, family members, coworkers, or other loved ones, they can all be a part of your support system. Don't forget to share with them your goals and motivations for following this diet. There will be days when intermittent fasting will be a breeze, whereas others will feel like an uphill battle. On days like these, your support system will grant you the motivation you need to keep going. If possible, find a dieting buddy. When you have someone else going through the same, the chances of sticking to the diet will increase. Also, it becomes fun. Today, several online support groups and chat rooms are available as well. You can use these platforms to connect with others who are following similar dietary protocols. Exchanging tips and sharing your experiences can help you push through and make you feel better and more confident about the diet.

Prioritize Protein Intake

Regardless of what you wish to eat or not, be sure to consume plenty of protein and complex carbs. These two food categories promote satiety and provide your body with all the nutrients needed. They are also relatively low in calories. There will be days when you feel like breaking the fast earlier or binging on something unhealthy. On days like these, consume all the required macros and essential nutrients before reaching for something sweet. This also reduces the risk of overeating. Fill yourself up with lean meat, lentils, legumes, healthy vegetables, and other forms of protein before succumbing to junk food. Once your hunger is satiated, the craving will automatically fade away.

Alternatively, you can also follow the delayed gratification technique to ensure that you don't give in to your cravings. The idea is quite simple: whenever a craving strikes you, take a break, breathe deeply, slowly sip on a glass of water, and make a note of your craving. Maintain a list of different foods you want to eat. Whenever you want to eat something, write it down. This simple act of expressing what you desire takes away some of the power the craving has over you. This also increases the chances of following a diet without any slip-ups.

Whenever you eat, make sure that you do not skimp on portion size. Remember, your body needs sufficient calories to function efficiently and effectively. If you starve yourself while fasting all day long, it does not promote weight loss. Instead, you will just end up doing more harm than good.

Plan to Deal with Hunger Pangs

One of the most common culprits for why people tend to give up on diets is hunger. Hunger pangs can quickly derail even the most motivated dieters. You should not only expect hunger pangs but prepare for them, too. You can tackle these spurs of hunger by adding calorie-free beverages, consuming more whole foods and satiating meals, or practicing delayed gratification. Perhaps the simplest one is to keep yourself busy. After all, if your brain is thoroughly engaged, whether it's working, reading, or enjoying music, you won't get a chance to think about your next meal.

Following the simple and practical advice in this chapter, jumping on the intermittent fasting bandwagon will be easier than ever.

Chapter 8: How to Keep Motivated While Fasting

It goes without saying that motivation is important in every aspect of life. The one difference between those who succeed and those trying to "make it" is their motivation. Internal motivation grants you the energy and reasons to keep going despite all obstacles and hurdles. In this section, let's look at a couple of simple tips you can follow to keep yourself motivated while following intermittent fasting.

Make a List of Your Goals

Goals give you a sense of purpose and direction. Without goals, chances are you will never get anywhere you want to be. Whether it's your personal or professional life, goals are necessary, and dieting is no exception. Now, before you start dieting, you need to understand your reasons for doing so. If you have no reason, what is the point of making all these changes? Make a list of all the different goals you want to achieve; be it weight loss and regulation or improving your overall state of health. You can have multiple goals. Once you have a few goals, list them in order of priority.

While setting goals, make sure they are SMART: Small, Measurable, Attainable, Relevant, and Time-bound. Unless all these elements are present, the chances of accomplishing those goals are reduced. Not setting goals is as dangerous as setting vague ones. For instance, a vague goal would be, "I want to lose weight." Instead, a good and clearly defined goal is, "I want to lose fifteen pounds within four months." This goal is doable and realistic. It also has a time limit, which will lower the chances of procrastination creeping in.

Have an Accountability Partner

It is a natural human tendency to behave or act according to what you say. Before you start the diet, talk to your support team about the diet and why you're following it. In a way, you are creating an external source of accountability. Now that you have shared your dreams and goals with someone else, the pressure to achieve those goals and to prove yourself become quite high. This is where accountability comes into play. Yes, you are personally accountable for yourself and your achievements, but external accountability works better.

If possible, find an accountability partner. Keeping track of your progress and sharing it with one person daily can be a positive and motivating experience. Enlisting a friend or an accountability buddy while you are getting started on this new journey will increase your likelihood of success. In today's world, we are all connected through the Internet, so regardless of where your accountability buddy is, you can always reach them with ease. If you want, you can also join an online community to that end.

Establish Short-Term Goals

We just mentioned that you need to establish certain goals for yourself while dieting. Now, it is time to establish a few short-term goals. Remember that any long-term objective can be easily broken down into multiple short-term goals. It's easier to achieve short-term goals, and every success that comes your way increases your motivation to keep going. After all, a long-term goal is nothing more than a combination and amalgamation of several short-term milestones. For instance, if you want to lose 15 lbs in four months, this can be further broken down into short-term goals. Like, "Following the intermittent fasting protocol for seven days straight" or "Exercising daily for thirty minutes." By breaking down the long-term objective into short-term goals, achieving the goal seems more realistic, practical, and achievable.

It isn't just important to establish goals but to decide on the rewards for attaining them, too. Why achieve a goal if there is no reward down the line? The rewards can be anything you want, except food! If the reward is food-related, it will soon undo all the benefits of fasting. Instead, it could be something like treating yourself to a manicure, buying those clothes you have meant to, or going out for a long drive. Whatever the activity is, make sure that you treat yourself to it after achieving each of your short-term goals.

Inspiring Content

The human brain is incredibly powerful, and you need to be mindful of all that you feed it. In our modern, ultra-connected world, we are constantly surrounded by information. If you don't start filtering what you're feeding your brain, it will quickly be overwhelmed. Your brain regulates your level of motivation. The simplest way to make sure you are highly motivated while following this diet is by feeding it motivational content. There is no need to do this for hours and hours; even ten minutes dedicated to feeding your brain quality inspirational content can do wonders. From watching YouTube videos and listening to podcasts to reading, there are many options available.

At times, especially when making a dietary change, it might not be easy, and you might feel all alone in your journey. These thoughts can quickly derail you and prevent you from fasting. As a guiding principle, no one is truly alone unless they believe it; others will always experience similar situations. So, dedicate a little time to read about others and their journeys, struggles, and successes.

Alternatively, turn your goals into positive affirmations and repeat them daily for five minutes, like a mantra. This is a simple exercise that can boost your motivation. Start your day with a couple of positive affirmations, and your motivation levels will stay high.

The Carrot and the Stick

Even the rewards may not seem that tempting or enticing enough to follow a diet. What can you do in these situations? Now, it's time for the carrot and the stick approach. This is a very simple technique, thanks to the analogy it uses. According to this technique, to motivate a donkey to move further along, you can either motivate it with a carrot or strike it with a stick. It implies motivation through reward or punishment. Punishment doesn't mean physically punishing yourself; it could be a sense of deprivation that acts as punishment. For instance, reward yourself with a spa day if you follow the diet for a whole month. Now, what would be the punishment if you do not achieve this goal? Perhaps you can eliminate one of your favorite foods from your diet for a couple of weeks. Or maybe increase the time spent working out. The idea of having to do something you don't want to can push you further and motivate you to do better.

Creative Visualization

Forget about establishing rewards or punishments for motivating yourself for a moment. Instead, there is another simple technique you can use, known as positive visualizations. In this technique, you close your eyes and picture a specific outcome or a scenario in your mind's eye. Visualization triggers your imagination, creativity, and jogs your memories. In parallel, it can tingle all your senses and awaken you from the inside. The next time you are running low on motivation, close your eyes and take a break from whatever you are doing for five minutes. Visualize how your life will be once you have attained your goals. How will you feel once you are fitter, healthier, or at your ideal body weight? How do you feel about yourself? How does life feel? Thinking about these questions and answering them honestly will provide several reasons why following the diet is desirable and the "right thing to do." This also gives you the instant motivation to keep going.

While using visualization, you can also use it to contemplate whether you are on the right path. For instance, close your eyes, and visualize how your life will be in the next six or twelve months if you quit the diet right now. It helps you take stock of your life and concentrate on making healthy and desirable changes voluntarily. If you are not willing to make these changes, following the diet will quickly become unbearable in the long run. Unless it comes from within, no one else can compel or force you.

Set fifteen minutes aside to reflect on your goals and where you want to be in life. You can also use positive affirmations that are meaningful to you and practice them daily. Managing your motivation levels is not difficult, provided you are interested and invested in doing so.

Focus on the Positives

Apart from visualizing a bright and healthy future, concentrate on the immediate positive aspects of fasting. This diet is bound to make you feel more confident, energetic, and productive. Whenever you attain a small goal, your motivation levels will increase. If you have never followed a diet before, imagine how you will feel if you follow intermittent fasting for ten days. If you have never exercised for a day in your life before, imagine the happiness of realizing that you have completed two weeks at the gym. These are the small positives associated with intermittent fasting. All it takes is a little time and commitment from you to see all the wonderful results it offers.

Focus on each of the positive feelings you experience daily while following this diet. It can be something as simple as saying no to dessert after eating or not adding sugar to your morning cup of coffee. You might not consciously think about these things or believe they are significant achievements, but they are. Every little positive step you take matters immensely. By celebrating them, your motivation and commitment will go through the roof.

Be Compassionate

You need to be compassionate, not just to others, but toward yourself as well. There will be days when you don't feel motivated, and it feels like an uphill battle. You probably realize the week or month ahead will not go according to what you might have planned. Instead of indulging in pointless negative talk, it's time to become mindful of your inner critic. Engaging in self-criticism and negative self-talk is quite easy, but this won't take you far.

On the contrary, finding something positive to concentrate on is seldom easy. If you want to attain your long-term objectives, it is important to tame your inner critic. Rather than focus solely on everything that isn't going right, concentrate on the good.

Apart from this, turn all the negative talk into positive self-talk. If you feel demotivated that you cannot get through the fasting window, tell yourself you possess the inner strength to complete the fast. By showing a little compassion toward yourself and being aware of your own strengths and weaknesses, your motivation levels will also increase.

Check Your Progress

Lastly, one important thing you need to do is continually check the progress you make. Even if it is just a week, there will be progress. Whether it is a slight fluctuation in your body weight or a general feeling of improvement in your life, there are different ways to check your progress. You will learn more about all this in the next chapter. For now, it is crucial to understand that motivation is something that is well within your control. No one else can motivate you unless you find that spark within. Another great thing about motivation is it increases your self-awareness.

Chapter 9: Non-Scale Victories and Fasting Setbacks

We just mentioned how important it is to measure the progress you make while fasting. Measuring progress is vital in order to understand the distance you've covered in life. Victories are not always measurable, and wins such as getting through a fasting day without thinking of giving up are also progress. Generally speaking, you cannot achieve success without failure. You will inevitably run into obstacles. You should not only expect this but must prepare yourself for it as well. When you are prepared, dealing with any potential setbacks becomes more manageable. In this chapter, you will learn about certain "non-scale victories" you should pay attention to and how to deal with setbacks throughout your intermittent fasting journey.

Non-Scale Victories to Celebrate

Whether you want to lose weight or lead a healthier life, none of this is going to be an overnight journey. It is a multifaceted process that requires sustained commitment and the development of healthier and more desirable habits. Non-scale victories, or NSVs, are simple health improvements resulting from small changes to your daily lifestyle. If the scale is your measure of success, you will forget all the small victories that come every step of the way. It is rather unfair that your journey to a healthier life and its efforts are reduced to a mere number on a scale. The number on the scale does not and cannot reflect all the changes you have made in your daily life. In this section, let us look at some simple non-scale victories most people forget to celebrate.

While following the 16/8 intermittent fasting protocol, chances are you will start feeling more energetic than you ever did. You are essentially consuming a healthy diet, exercising regularly, and getting sufficient sleep. Combining all these factors makes it abundantly clear how a simple diet can make you feel more energetic. By feeding your body all the nutrients and physical activity it needs to function effectively, its overall productivity and efficiency is guaranteed to improve.

Perhaps the most important non-scale victory you need to pay attention to is how your clothes fit. Even if there is no dip or fluctuation in your weight on the scale, chances are your clothes will fit you better after two weeks of intermittent fasting. At times, weight loss isn't always visible. This is especially true for fat loss. When your clothes fit better, you can see that this diet is working and delivering the expected results. According to the research conducted by Courtney Maclin-Akinyemi et al. (2017), among 77% of women and over 35% of men who wanted to lose weight, their clothes fitted them better. So, start paying attention to how your clothes fit as you advance through the fasting protocol.

If you have successfully shifted to an intermittent fasting lifestyle, chances are your sleep pattern has also improved. When you have a proper schedule in place and are sticking to it, it becomes easier to tire your body and brain out at the end of the day. For instance, exercising regularly is believed to regulate your internal sleep cycle. Even losing body fat has a positive effect on sleep and its quality.

According to the research conducted by Soohyun Nam et al. (2018), weight loss can improve your quality of sleep over time.

It isn't secret knowledge that exercise has multiple health benefits. If you exercise more than you ever did, your fitness will improve, and you might not have even noticed it yet. Slowly, you will notice that you can exercise for longer, perform more reps, and even lift heavier weights. All these changes are an indication that you are progressing in the right direction. When the intensity and duration of exercise increases gradually, it shows you that your body has come a long way. This is a fitness milestone that you have attained—do not forget to celebrate it.

According to a study by Nicola Veronese et al. (2017), weight loss can improve your memory, increase your attention span, and support quicker mental processing. This goes to show that any improvement in your physical health will assist your cognitive functioning, too.

A wonderful thing about intermittent fasting is it promotes the concept of healthy and wholesome eating instead of mindlessly bingeing on processed foods. By eliminating all undesirable food from your diet, such as those rich in trans fats and unhealthy sugars, and by replacing them with healthier fruit, vegetables, and wholesome ingredients, there will be a positive effect. According to the study conducted by Rajani Katta et al. (2014), your skin's health can improve when you limit dairy products and high glycemic index foods. Since intermittent fasting encourages the consumption of fruit and vegetables rich in antioxidants and a variety of nutrients and vitamins, this will promote visibly clearer and smoother skin over time.

Perhaps the most important non-scale victory you need to celebrate is when you have lost inches. If you are exercising daily by engaging in weight or strength training, your body measurements will change. As such, one of the most important numbers you need to keep track of is your waist circumference. Before you start this diet, measure yourself and make a list of your body measurements. Also, monitor your waist to hip ratio. All the healthy, desirable lifestyle habits and changes (and sacrifices) you are making now will certainly pay off.

Let's not forget that your emotional state affects your eating patterns. If you take a moment and think about it, this makes perfect sense. Chances are you feel like eating something sweet when you're feeling sad, something crunchy when you're upset, or junk food when you're bored. This is because of dopamine released in the brain, a chemical associated with the "feel-good" or reward feeling. Stress eating is also referred to as emotional eating, and it activates the "eat and reward" connection in your brain. If you no longer reach for food to cope with any stress you are experiencing, it is an important victory that you cannot ignore.

As you start losing weight, the stress on your muscles and joints will diminish. This is especially true for the weight-bearing ones in your back and legs. With weight loss, your joint pain will also be reduced. This, in turn, makes it easier to become more physically active and fit, which will promote further weight loss.

One healthy lifestyle change that intermittent fasting will introduce you to is home cooking. Cooking at home can be incredibly fun and exciting once you start following the different recipes provided in this book. It also gives you better control over your body's nutritional requirements and the cooking process. Combined, these factors are bound to improve your relationship with food. Another notable benefit of cooking at home regularly is that it will lighten your financial expenses. If you are used to ordering take-out or other convenience foods, you have probably been spending a lot more than you realized. Your bank balance will certainly thank you once you start cooking at home! You can also set aside a monthly food budget to accommodate all your dietary needs and requirements without any hassle.

Another non-scale victory is an improvement in your overall mood. When you start eating better, exercising regularly, and sleeping through the night like a baby, your mood will automatically improve. As mentioned earlier, if you have recognized any emotional eating patterns and managed to hit a breakthrough, you can now handle stress without reaching for food. Combining all these essential elements will automatically make you feel better about yourself and everything you undertake. When your mood is better, your overall performance and productivity will also skyrocket.

In parallel, you need to regularly check certain health markers such as blood sugar and blood pressure. In the previous chapter, you were introduced to the various benefits of intermittent fasting and scientific evidence that backs these claims. If you regularly follow the protocol, do not forget to check your blood sugar and blood pressure levels. If you notice an improvement in both of these health markers, it means the diet is working for you.

Losing weight can be a health goal in itself. Measuring weight loss from time to time is perfectly normal. Still, as established, this is not the only means to determine your success while dieting. Most of the non-scale victories discussed in this section may not reflect in your weight, but they're worth celebrating. With every little win that comes your way, your motivation for following this diet will increase. When you know you are making healthy changes and they are paying off, you will feel better.

Fasting Setbacks to Tackle

You can lose weight and keep it off with intermittent fasting. This is perhaps the most common reason why people turn to this diet. By fasting for sixteen hours, your body's metabolism increases and accelerates weight loss. You may be wondering what the common weight loss benefit offered by this diet is. Diets take time to show results. This stands true for intermittent fasting, too. As long as you follow this diet for at least eight to ten weeks, you will witness positive changes. During this period, you can expect to lose anywhere between 6-10 lbs. The journey of weight loss is not an overnight process; you did not gain all those excess pounds overnight, so how can you lose them immediately? Different factors come into play when it comes to weight loss. Your gender, level of activity, and dietary choices will command your weight loss journey.

Do not compare your weight loss results with someone else and feel bad (remember, no negative self-perception!). Realize that the results will vary from one person to another. If you are not losing weight, chances are something isn't right in your diet planning or execution. In this upcoming section, let's look at some fasting setbacks and how you can tackle them efficiently.

Eating Too Much after Fasting

Perhaps the most common mistake many people make when they start fasting is that they overeat once their eating window starts. Don't think of the eating window as the timeframe to compensate for the fasting period. If weight loss is your priority, your calorie expenditure needs to exceed your calorie intake. If you consume more calories during the eating window than before intermittent fasting, you won't notice any weight loss. If all the calories you normally consume were shifted to the eating period, this diet would not make any sense.

Instead of eating too much, eat until you are full. To do this, adopt the habit of eating slowly, chewing thoroughly, and making healthier dietary choices. Putting your fork down between each bite can also help if you're a fast eater. Unless you do all this, you cannot see positive change. If you want, you can also use a calorie counting app during the initial days to make healthier choices. No, you don't have to count every calorie you ingest, but becoming aware of what you eat will help with weight loss.

Not Eating Nutritious Food

We've established and reiterated that intermittent fasting protocols are more about when you eat than what you eat. Intermittent fasting should not become your excuse for eating whatever you want during the eating window. If weight loss is your goal, consuming calorie-dense foods such as prepackaged and processed junk food will not promote weight loss (quite the opposite). Instead, your primary focus should be nutrient-dense foods. You were introduced to various foods you can safely consume during intermittent fasting in the previous section. Fill up on healthy fats, lean protein, and fiber-rich carbohydrates to reduce your overall calorie intake and promote satiety. It doesn't mean you need to deprive yourself of the foods you love and enjoy. As long as treats like chocolate and ice cream are occasional and within reasonable limits, you don't have to deprive yourself of anything.

Skipping Meals during the Eating Window

If you don't eat sufficient food during the eating window, sustaining your body through fasting quickly becomes difficult. If you starve yourself pointlessly by skipping meals, it increases hunger pangs, making it more difficult to stick to your schedule. Restricting yourself too much also increases the risk of overeating or bingeing on unhealthy foods when your fasting window ends. Apart from all this, you are depriving your body of the essential nutritients it requires. Remember, it was mentioned that shifting to starvation mode is never ideal. Once your body is in the starvation stage, it stops burning calories and instead starts protecting and harboring them. This can result in weight gain rather than weight loss.

Do not overindulge during the eating window. Instead, you need to eat until your hunger is satisfied. Doing a little meal prep on the weekends makes it easier to prepare the required meals during the week since most of the work is already done. When you know a meal is ready and waiting for you, the chances of getting thrown off schedule are dramatically reduced.

Not Fasting Long Enough

There will be days when it feels like you cannot complete the entire sixteen hours of fasting. On days like these, listen to your body, but don't make a habit of it. You need to fast for sixteen hours if you want to see the positive results promised by this diet. If you regularly skip fasting, what good is trying in the first place? If you want to reap the benefits of this diet, you need to fast for at least fourteen hours daily. By following the schedule, you slowly get your body accustomed to eating during a specific window and fasting for the rest of the day. After that, all that is required is commitment and self-control.

You Are Not Sleeping Properly

The importance of sleep should never be overlooked when it comes to improving and maintaining your overall health and wellbeing. Sleep not only awards your body the rest it needs, but it affects your metabolism. Improper sleep increases certain hunger-inducing hormones, which makes it difficult to stick to the fasting schedule. Also, when you sleep, your body finally gets a chance to work on actively digesting whatever you have consumed during the eating window. Make an effort to sleep for at least seven to eight hours daily. It is not just the duration of the sleep that matters; quality is just as important. You need to get good quality sleep every night, which can be promoted by a warm shower and aromatherapy.

Not Drinking Enough Water

Drinking plenty of water and staying hydrated can never be underestimated. This point has been repeatedly stressed in this book because dehydration is quite common, and many people forget about it. Another important benefit of drinking sufficient water is that it quells hunger. At times, you may feel hungry, only to realize that a big cup of water is all you needed.

Exercising Too Much

It can be quite tempting to exercise more vigorously and for longer while shifting to this diet. After all, exercising is important for weight loss and maintenance in general. Unfortunately, it doesn't help—at least initially—so don't go overboard and don't push your body beyond its limits. Exercising too hard and not eating enough is a recipe for disaster. Instead of attaining your weight loss goals, it will harm your body and health in the long run. Over-exercising or working out more intensively than required while reducing food intake will augment your hunger and reduce your energy levels. As a result, you may also overeat and binge on unhealthy calories. During the initial couple of days, make sure your exercise routine is quite light. Once your body is accustomed to fasting, you can gradually increase the intensity of your workout routine. Remember, this is a long-term plan and not an overnight process.

Lack of Planning

One of the most common mistakes people make while shifting to intermittent fasting is that they don't plan. You need to plan, and there is no way around it. As we've seen, coming up with an intermittent fasting schedule is not a Herculean task. Once you target your lifestyle needs and requirements, simply adjust them according to this diet. If you keep cutting corners or cheating on your meal plan from one week to another, the yields will not be worth the effort you exert. Consistency is fundamental because intermittent fasting is more of a lifestyle than just another diet. Plan all your meals and snacks. Prepare a few snacks and meals and keep them handy. Also, don't forget to stock your pantry with the required nutrient-dense ingredients. This makes following the diet a breeze. It also gives you enough flexibility to decide what you want to eat and switch things up from time to time.

Feeling Guilty

Be patient and consistent in your efforts while shifting to intermittent fasting. There will be days when you need to break your fast ahead of schedule, or ones when you cannot fast at all. If you want to follow this diet, make it sustainable, and uphold your commitment, then you should not feel guilty or ashamed when you cannot complete the fast. These negative feelings can prevent you from getting back on track the following day. There will be setbacks, inevitably, but it's best to focus on your commitment. It is okay if you cannot complete your fast one day. As long as you start fasting the next day, you have nothing to worry about. Cut yourself some slack, and don't take these setbacks personally. Instead, concentrate on your journey and all the progress you are making.

At the end of the day, progress is impossible without setbacks. So, don't get discouraged, and instead, follow the simple steps and suggestions given in this chapter to make things easier.

Chapter 10: Intermittent Fasting 16/8 Recipes and Meal Plan

Meal Shakes

Peanut Butter Cup Shake

Number of servings: 2

Nutritional values per serving:

Calories – 260

Fat – 6 grams

Carbohydrates – 21 grams

Protein – 30 grams

Ingredients:

- 1 cup unsweetened almond milk
- 2 tablespoons cocoa powder
- 1 tablespoon natural peanut butter
- 2 scoops vanilla or chocolate plant-based protein powder
- 1 frozen banana, sliced

- Water, as required (optional)

Directions:

1. Pour almond milk into the blender. Add cocoa, peanut butter, protein powder, and banana.
2. Blend until you get a smooth puree.
3. If the shake looks too thick, add water and blend until smooth. You can add ice as well.
4. Pour into two tall glasses and serve.

Dark Chocolate Peppermint Shake

Number of servings: 2

Nutritional values per serving:

Calories – 295

Fat – 6 grams

Carbohydrates – 49 grams

Protein – 22 grams

Ingredients:

- 2 large frozen bananas, sliced
- 2 cups non-dairy milk of your preference
- 4 tablespoons cocoa powder
- 2 tablespoons dark chocolate chips (optional)
- 2 scoops of whey chocolate protein powder
- ½ teaspoon pure peppermint extract
- Ice cubes, as required
- 1/8 teaspoon salt

Directions:

1. Place banana, cocoa, protein powder, salt, and peppermint extract into the blender.
2. Pour milk and blend the mixture until nice and smooth. Add dark chocolate chips if you are using them and blend until smooth.
3. Add ice cubes and blend once again.
4. Enjoy the shake in tall glasses.

Strawberry Cheesecake Shake

Number of servings: 2

Nutritional values per serving:

Calories - 210

Fat - 5 grams

Carbohydrates - 7 grams

Protein - 30 grams

Ingredients:

- 2 cups almond milk
- 2/3 cup whey protein powder
- 1 cup frozen strawberries
- 2 tablespoons light cream cheese

Directions:

1. Pour almond milk into the blender. Add protein powder, strawberries, and cream cheese.
2. Blend for few seconds until you get a smooth puree.
3. Pour into two tall glasses and serve.

Very Berry Super Shake

Number of servings: 1

Nutritional values per serving:

Calories – 500

Fat – 11 grams

Carbohydrates – 54 grams

Protein – 57 grams

Ingredients:

- ¾ cup water
- 1 cup frozen mixed berries
- 1 scoop vanilla protein powder
- ½ tablespoon ground flaxseeds
- ½ cup spinach
- ¼ cup plain, low-fat yogurt
- ½ tablespoon walnuts

Directions:

1. Place berries, water, vanilla protein powder, flaxseeds, spinach, yogurt, and walnuts into a blender.
2. Blend the mixture until you get a smooth puree.
3. Pour into a tall glass and serve.

Pineapple Green Smoothie

Number of servings: 2

Nutritional values per serving:

Calories - 295

Fat - 5.5 grams

Carbohydrates - 54 grams

Protein - 13 grams

Ingredients:

- 1 cup unsweetened almond milk
- 2 cups baby spinach
- 1 cup frozen pineapple chunks
- 2 - 7 teaspoons pure maple syrup or honey (optional)
- 2/3 cup nonfat, plain Greek yogurt
- 2 medium frozen bananas, sliced
- 2 tablespoons chia seeds

Directions:

1. Pour yogurt and almond milk into the blender. Place spinach, chia seeds, pineapple, banana, and maple syrup into the blender.

2. Keep blending until you get a smooth puree.

3. Pour into two tall glasses and serve.

Strawberry Chocolate Smoothie

Number of servings: 2

Nutritional values per serving:

Calories – 305

Fat – 13.4 grams

Carbohydrates – 46.8 grams

Protein – 7.4 grams

Ingredients:

- 3 cups frozen strawberries
- 2 tablespoons almond butter
- 2 tablespoons honey
- 2 cups chilled, unsweetened, chocolate almond milk
- 2 tablespoons unsweetened cocoa powder

Directions:

1. Place strawberries and cocoa powder into the blender. Add honey and milk. Then add the almond butter.

2. Blend until nice and smooth. Once smooth, pour into two glasses and serve.

Carrot Apple Smoothie

Number of servings: 1

Nutritional values per serving:

Calories - 245

Fat - 8 grams

Carbohydrates - 46 grams

Protein - 4 grams

Ingredients:

- 1 large carrot, sliced
- ½ large honey crisp apple, cored, cut in two
- 1 tablespoon fresh lemon juice
- 1 teaspoon minced fresh turmeric or ½ teaspoon turmeric powder
- ½ medium ripe banana, sliced
- ½ cup light coconut milk
- 1 teaspoon minced fresh ginger
- Ice cubes, as required

Directions:

1. Pour coconut milk into the blender. Add ginger, carrot, turmeric, apple, lemon juice, and banana.

2. Blitz until you get a smooth puree. Now add the ice cubes and blend.

3. Pour into a tall glass and serve.

Mango Raspberry Smoothie

Number of servings: 2

Nutritional values per serving:

Calories – 190

Fat – 7.4 grams

Carbohydrates – 32 grams

Protein – 1.5 grams

Ingredients:

- 1 cup water
- 2 tablespoons lemon juice
- ½ cup frozen raspberries
- ½ medium avocado, peeled, pitted, chopped
- 1 ½ cups frozen mango
- 2 tablespoons agave nectar

Directions:

1. Place avocado, mango, lemon juice, agave nectar, and raspberries into a blender. Pour water and blitz until you get a smooth puree.

2. Pour into two tall glasses and serve with crushed ice if desired.

Strawberry Oat Smoothie

Number of servings: 2

Nutritional values per serving:

Calories – 280

Fat – 2 grams

Carbohydrates – 56 grams

Protein – 13 grams

Ingredients:

- 2 cups sliced strawberries
- 2 cups nonfat milk
- 2 teaspoons honey
- Ice cubes, as required
- 1 banana, sliced
- ½ cup rolled oats
- ½ teaspoon vanilla extract

Directions:

1. Place oats, strawberries, honey, ice cubes, vanilla, and banana into a blender.
2. Pour milk on top and blitz until you get a smooth puree.
3. Pour into two tall glasses and serve.

Raspberry Peanut Butter Smoothie

Number of servings: 2

Nutritional values per serving:

Calories - 270

Fat - 12 grams

Carbohydrates - 38 grams

Protein - 7 grams

Ingredients:

- 1 banana, sliced
- 2 cups almond milk
- 1 cup ice as required
- 2 cups raspberries
- 2 tablespoons peanut butter

Directions:

1. Place banana, almond milk, ice, raspberries, and peanut butter into the blender.
2. Blend until you get a smooth puree.
3. Pour into two glasses and serve.

Flax Seed Smoothie

Number of servings: 2

Nutritional values per serving:

Calories - 275

Fat - 8 grams

Carbohydrates - 47 grams

Protein - 7.5 grams

Ingredients:

- 1 frozen banana, sliced
- 4 tablespoons flaxseed meal
- 2 cups frozen strawberries
- 2 cups low-fat vanilla soymilk

Directions:

1. Place strawberries, banana slices, and flaxseed meal into a blender.

2. Pour soymilk on top. Blitz until you get a smooth puree.

3. Pour into two tall glasses. Serve with crushed ice if desired.

Breakfast Recipes

Veggie Mini Quiches

Number of servings: 3

Nutritional values per serving: (4 mini quiches)

Calories - 95

Fat - 6.8 grams

Carbohydrates - 2 grams

Protein - 6 grams

Ingredients:

- 1 teaspoon coconut oil
- 1 medium carrot, grated
- 2 large eggs, whisked
- Salt to taste
- 1/3 heaped cup zucchini
- 1 green onion, finely chopped (keep the greens and whites separate)
- 3 tablespoons grated Monterrey Jack cheese

Directions:

1. Take a mini cupcake pan and spray cooking spray into the wells. You need to spray oil into 12 of the wells.
2. Take a skillet and keep it over medium flame. Pour oil into the skillet and let it heat.
3. Once the oil is heated, add whites of the green onion, carrots, and zucchini and stir-fry for a few minutes until the vegetables are soft. Turn off the heat and stir in the greens of the green onion. Let cool completely.
4. Crack the eggs into a bowl and beat well. Add the sautéed vegetables, salt, and cheese and stir.
5. Pour the egg mixture into the prepared muffin pan.

6. Bake the mini quiches in an oven that has been preheated to 350°F, for about 15-18 minutes or until the eggs are set.

7. Let the mini quiches cool in the pan for 15 minutes. Take a knife and run it around the edges of the quiches to loosen them from the mold.

8. The mini quiches are ready to serve now.

Ham, Egg, and Avocado Breakfast Burrito

Number of servings: 4

Nutritional values per serving:

Calories – 400

Fat – 24 grams

Carbohydrates – 36 grams

Protein – 16 grams

Ingredients:

- 4 eggs
- 1 cup cooked, diced ham
- 4 large whole wheat tortillas
- 2 tablespoons milk
- 2 avocadoes, peeled, pitted, sliced
- Grated cheese

Directions:

1. Beat eggs in a microwave-safe greased bowl. Add milk and whisk well.
2. Place the bowl in the microwave and cook on high for about a minute. Stir the eggs and place them back in the microwave. Continue cooking until the eggs are set.
3. Make four equal portions of the eggs, avocado, ham, and cheese. Scatter one portion of each, along the diameter of each of the tortillas.
4. Wrap the tortillas like a burrito. The burritos are ready to serve.
5. If desired, you can also cook the burritos in a skillet or a Panini press until golden brown. The choice is yours.

Cauliflower English Muffins

Number of servings: 8

Nutritional values per serving: (2 muffins per serving, without toppings)

Calories - 170

Fat - 11 grams

Carbohydrates - 7.5 grams

Protein - 10.5 grams

Ingredients:

- 10 cups cauliflower florets (around 2 pounds)
- 2 large eggs, lightly beaten
- 2 cups sharp cheddar cheese
- ¼ teaspoon salt

Directions:

1. Take two large baking trays and place a sheet of parchment paper on each.
2. Process the cauliflower in the food processor until you get a rice-like texture.
3. Place the cauliflower rice in a microwave-safe bowl. Cover the bowl loosely and cook the cauliflower on High in a microwave for 4 minutes.
4. Take a large piece of kitchen cloth. Place cauliflower on the center of the cloth. Bring the edges of the cloth together and squeeze the cauliflower to remove extra moisture.
5. Place the squeezed cauliflower in a bowl along with eggs, cheddar cheese, and salt and mix until well combined.
6. Take a 3-inch biscuit cutter and place it on one corner of the baking sheet. Place about ¼ cup of the cauliflower mixture inside the cutter. Press lightly and carefully remove the biscuit cutter.

7. Leave a one-inch gap and repeat this process. When the baking sheet is full, place the cauliflower similarly on the other baking sheet. You should have 16 muffins in total.

8. Place the baking tray in an oven that has been preheated to 425°F for about 25-30 minutes or until you can see them browning around the edges.

9. You can use your own favorite toppings to serve the muffins. You can use them to make sandwiches as well.

Broccoli and Parmesan Cheese Omelet

Number of servings: 2

Nutritional values per serving: (1 omelet)

Calories – 410

Fat – 20 grams

Carbohydrates – 22 grams

Protein – 33 grams

Ingredients:

- 4 large egg whites
- 4 large eggs
- 2 teaspoons extra-virgin olive oil
- 2 shallots, finely chopped
- 2 slices sprouted grain bread
- 1 cup chopped broccoli
- ½ cup finely grated parmesan cheese

Directions:

1. Place eggs and egg whites in a bowl and whisk well.
2. Pour oil into a small skillet and heat over medium flame. Once the oil is heated, add shallots and broccoli and cook until the broccoli turns bright green.
3. Remove half the broccoli mixture from the pan and place it in a bowl.
4. Spread the remaining broccoli mixture all over the skillet.
5. Pour half the egg mixture into the pan, all over the broccoli, making sure not to stir.
6. Scatter half the cheese on top. Cook covered until the eggs are cooked. Remove omelet onto a plate.
7. Make the other omelet using the broccoli mixture that was set aside, the remaining cheese, and the remaining egg mixture.

8. Meanwhile, toast the bread slices the desired amount.

9. To assemble: place a slice of toast on individual serving plates.

10. Place an omelet on each piece of toast and serve. You can fold the omelet in half or a quarter before placing it on the toast.

Summer Skillet Vegetable and Egg Scramble

Number of servings: 2

Nutritional values per serving: (1-½ cups portion)

Calories – 255

Fat – 14 grams

Carbohydrates – 19.5 grams

Protein – 12.5 grams

Ingredients:

- 1 tablespoon olive oil
- 2 cups thinly sliced mixed vegetables (mushroom, zucchini, and bell pepper)
- ½ teaspoon minced fresh herbs of your choice
- 1 cup packed baby kale or baby spinach
- 6 ounces baby potatoes, thinly sliced
- 1 ½ scallions, thinly sliced (keep the greens and whites separate)
- 3 large eggs, lightly beaten
- ¼ teaspoon salt or to taste

Directions:

1. Pour oil into a large skillet and heat over medium flame. When the oil is heated, add potatoes and stir.

2. Keep the skillet covered and cook until slightly soft. Make sure you stir often.

3. Stir in mixed vegetables and whites of the scallions and cook until vegetables are light brown and slightly soft.

4. Add the fresh herbs and stir. Push the vegetables to the edges of the skillet.

5. Lower the heat to medium-low. Place scallion greens in the center of the skillet. Add eggs over the scallion greens and stir. Cook until the eggs are soft-cooked, stirring often.

6. Add kale into the egg mixture and stir. Turn off the heat.

7. Now mix the egg scramble and the vegetables. Add salt and stir.

8. Divide onto two plates and serve.

Loaded Baked Potato Breakfast Casserole

Number of servings: 4

Nutritional values per serving:

Calories - 165

Fat - 10 grams

Carbohydrates - 8 grams

Protein - 11 grams

Ingredients:

- 6 ounces baby potatoes
- ¼ cup light sour cream + extra for serving
- ¼ cup milk
- ½ cup chopped green bell pepper
- 2 thick slices bacon, cooked, crumbled + extra for serving
- 4 eggs
- ½ teaspoon salt
- ¼ cup shredded cheddar cheese + extra for serving
- 1 green onion, sliced + extra for serving
- Pepper to taste

Directions:

1. Prepare a baking sheet by lining it with aluminum foil. Place potatoes on the baking sheet.

2. Place the baking sheet in an oven that has been preheated to 400°F and bake for about 30 minutes or until the potatoes are cooked.

3. Take out the baking sheet from the oven and let the potatoes cool. Chop the potatoes into smaller pieces.

4. Now, set the oven temperature to 350°F and wait for the temperature to reduce.

5. Take a baking dish of about 6 - 7 inches or use a small casserole dish and grease it with cooking spray.

6. Beat the eggs in a bowl while adding milk, sour cream, and salt. Add potatoes, bacon, onion, bell pepper, and cheese and stir until well incorporated.

7. Transfer the mixture into the baking dish and place the dish in the oven.

8. Set the timer for about 30 minutes and let it bake until the eggs are cooked in the middle. If you see the edges are getting brown and the center is not cooked, cover the dish with foil and bake.

9. Garnish with green onion, bacon, and cheese. Drizzle sour cream on top and serve.

Layered Chia Pudding with Mixed Fruit Puree

Number of servings: 4

Nutritional values per serving: (1 glass)

Calories - 685

Fat - 35 grams

Carbohydrates - 74 grams

Protein - 24 grams

Ingredients:

For chia pudding:

- 1 cup chia seeds
- 2 teaspoons vanilla extract
- 4 cups almond milk or any other plant-based milk of your choice
- 2 tablespoons maple syrup

For parfait:

- 2 large mangoes, peeled, cubed
- 2 cups raspberries
- 4 kiwis, peeled, cubed
- 4 tablespoons yogurt or coconut yogurt or soy yogurt
- 4 tablespoons hemp hearts

Directions:

1. Combine almond milk, maple syrup, and vanilla extract in a bowl.

2. Stir in the chia seeds. Keep stirring for a couple of minutes.

3. Cover the bowl and keep the bowl in the refrigerator for about an hour or until thick.

4. While the pudding is chilling, prepare the fruit puree. For this, blend the kiwis in a blender. Once you get a smooth puree, pour it into a bowl.

5. Rinse the blender and now place mangoes into the blender. Blend the mangoes until you get a smooth puree.

6. Pour the mango puree into another bowl.

7. Rinse the blender, and now place the raspberries into the blender. Blend the raspberries until you get a smooth puree.

8. Pour the raspberry puree into a third bowl.

9. To assemble the pudding: Take four glasses and pour any one of the fruit purees into the glasses. Make sure that the puree is equally distributed among the glasses.

10. Divide half of the chia pudding among the glasses, and this will be your next layer.

11. Place a tablespoon of yogurt in each glass.

12. Next, pour another fruit puree into the glasses, again distributing equally among the glasses.

13. Divide the third puree equally among the glasses to create the final layer.

14. Sprinkle a tablespoon of hemp seeds on top of each glass.

15. You can serve right away or chill and serve later. If desired, you can garnish with fresh fruit before serving.

Choco-Chip and Banana Pancakes

Number of servings: 6

Nutritional values per serving: (1 pancake)

Calories – 250

Fat – 8 grams

Carbohydrates – 37 grams

Protein – 8 grams

Ingredients:

- 6 tablespoons white self-rising flour
- ½ cup whole-wheat self-rising flour
- 1 tablespoon sugar or coconut sugar or any other sweetener of your choice
- 1 teaspoon baking powder
- 1 overripe banana, mashed
- 1 egg
- ¾ cup + 1/8 cup low-fat or skim milk or almond milk
- 1 teaspoon vanilla extract
- 3 tablespoons chocolate chips
- 1 tablespoon light butter or coconut oil, melted or any other oil of your preference

Serving options:

- Maple syrup or any other syrup of your choice
- Berries
- Coconut butter or nut butter
- Fruit of your choice
- Whipped cream etc.

Directions:

1. Whisk together banana, sugar, vanilla, milk, and egg in a bowl. Add oil and whisk well.

2. Add flour and baking powder and whisk until just incorporated. Add milk and stir until just combined. Do not over-whisk.

3. Add chocolate chips and fold gently.

4. Place a nonstick pan over a medium flame. When the pan is heated, spray the pan with cooking spray. Pour about ¼ cup of batter on the pan. Swirl the pan to spread the pancake. Slowly bubbles will be visible on top. Cook until the underside is brown. Turn the pancake over and cook the other side as well.

5. Remove the pancake from the pan and keep warm.

6. Make the remaining pancakes, similarly, following steps 4 – 5.

7. Serve pancakes with any of the suggested serving options.

Sweet Potato Waffles

Number of servings: 8

Nutritional values per serving: (1 waffle without toppings)

Calories - 270

Fat - 5 grams

Carbohydrates - 52 grams

Protein - 6 grams

Ingredients:

- 1 cup canned sweet potato puree
- 2 tablespoons canola or light olive oil
- 2 tablespoons honey
- 1 cup milk
- 2 eggs
- 2 cups pancake or waffle mix

Directions:

1. Whisk together sweet potatoes, eggs, milk, oil, and honey in a bowl until smooth.
2. Stir in pancake mix using a wooden spoon. Stir until almost free from lumps.
3. Set up your waffle iron and preheat it following the directions of the manufacturer.
4. Pour 1/8 of the batter into the waffle iron. Close the lid and set the timer according to the manufacturer's instructions.
5. Once waffles are cooked, you can serve with toppings of your choice.
6. Cook the remaining waffles similarly. You can store leftover waffles in an airtight container in the refrigerator (good for up to three days). They can be frozen for up to 3 months.

Pink Breakfast Bowl

Number of servings: 2

Nutritional values per serving:

Calories - 365

Fat - 10 grams

Carbohydrates - 54 grams

Protein - 11 grams

Ingredients:

- 1 ½ cups cooked quinoa or millet or rice
- 2 tablespoons raw or lightly toasted seeds like pumpkin seeds or sunflower seeds, or chopped nuts
- 2 cups unsweetened nondairy milk of your choice
- 2 handfuls of dried fruit like raisins, goji berries, and chopped dates
- Hemp seeds to garnish (optional)
- 2 small beets, peeled, finely grated
- 2 tablespoons chia seeds
- 2 teaspoons ground cinnamon

Directions:

1. Combine the cooked quinoa and seeds, milk, beets, chia seeds, and cinnamon in a bowl.
2. Divide into 2 serving bowls.
3. Sprinkle hemp seeds and dried fruit on top and serve.

Chocolate Fudge Brownie Oatmeal

Number of servings: 2

Nutritional values per serving:

Calories - 355

Fat - 6 grams

Carbohydrates - 52 grams

Protein - 27 grams

Ingredients:

- 1 cup old fashioned rolled oats
- Truvia to taste (optional)
- 20 drops stevia extract or to taste
- ¼ cup dark cocoa powder
- 2 cups milk, divided
- 2 scoops of chocolate protein powder

Directions:

1. Place cocoa, oats, truvia, 1 ½ cups milk into a microwave-safe container. Keep stirring until the mixture thickens.

2. Place the container in the microwave and cook on high for about 3 minutes.

3. Combine stevia, ½ cup milk, and protein powder in a bowl. Whisk until free from lumps.

4. Pour into the bowl of oatmeal and keep stirring until well incorporated.

5. Divide into bowls and serve.

Lunch Recipes

Black Beans and Mango Salad

Number of servings: 6

Nutritional values per serving: (about 7 ounces)

Calories – 350

Fat – 1.5 grams

Carbohydrates – 70 grams

Protein – 17 grams

Ingredients:

- 16 ounces cooked or canned black beans
- 2 tablespoons fresh lemon juice
- 2 tablespoons fresh lime juice
- 2 tablespoons orange juice
- 1/3 cup chopped cilantro
- 20 ounces mango, peeled, cut into cubes
- Salt to taste
- 2 tablespoons maple syrup
- Pepper to taste

Directions:

1. Place black beans and mango in a bowl and toss well.
2. Whisk together lime juice, orange juice, and lemon juice in a bowl. Add maple syrup and whisk well. Stir in cilantro, salt, and pepper.
3. Pour over the bean mixture and toss well.
4. Cover the bowl and chill until use.
5. Divide into 6 bowls and serve.

Green Goddess Salad with Chicken

Number of servings: 2

Nutritional values per serving: (about 5 cups with 1 tablespoon of dressing)

Calories - 295

Fat - 7.5 grams

Carbohydrates - 14.5 grams

Protein - 43 grams

Ingredients:

For green goddess dressing:

- 2 avocadoes, peeled, pitted, chopped
- ½ cup fresh, chopped herbs of your choice (you may use a mixture of herbs as well)
- 1 teaspoon salt or to taste
- 3 cups buttermilk
- 4 tablespoons rice vinegar

For salad:

- 6 cups chopped romaine lettuce
- 6 ounces cooked, diced, skinless, boneless chicken breast
- 12 cherry tomatoes, halved
- 2 cups sliced cucumber
- 1 cup diced, low-fat Swiss cheese

Directions:

1. To make green goddess dressing: blend avocado, herbs, salt, buttermilk, and vinegar in a blender until you get a smooth puree. Pour into an airtight container and refrigerate until use. This should make around 3 ½ cups.

2. To serve: drizzle 2 tablespoons dressing over the salad. Stir until well combined.

3. Transfer into two serving bowls. Divide the chicken, tomatoes, and cheese among the bowls. You can add more dressing if desired, and the remaining dressing can be used in some other recipe. It can last for 3 - 4 days in the refrigerator.

4. Serve.

Cucumber Turkey Club Sandwich

Number of servings: 2

Nutritional values per serving: (1 sandwich)

Calories - 325

Fat - 18 grams

Carbohydrates - 15 grams

Protein - 26 grams

Ingredients:

- 2 large cucumbers, peeled, halved lengthwise
- 4 teaspoons mayonnaise
- 2 slices cheddar cheese or Swiss cheese
- 2 thin, round slices of onion
- 4 teaspoons yellow or brown deli mustard
- 4 ounces sliced deli turkey breast
- 6 thin, round slices of tomatoes
- Pepper to taste

Directions:

1. Take a spoon and carefully scoop the seeds from the cucumber halves. Discard the seeds.
2. Spread a teaspoon of mayonnaise and mustard on each half of the cucumber half on the cut side.
3. Place turkey slices on two of the cucumber halves. Layer with cheese, followed by tomatoes and onion. Season with pepper.
4. Complete the sandwich by covering with the remaining cucumber halves.
5. Cut each sandwich into two halves and serve.

Tuna and Chickpea Pita Sandwiches

Number of servings: 2

Nutritional values per serving: (1 sandwich)

Calories - 320

Fat - 8 grams

Carbohydrates - 36 grams

Protein - 23 grams

Ingredients:

For dressing:

- 3 tablespoons fat-free or low-fat Greek yogurt
- 1 ¼ tablespoons fresh lemon juice or to taste
- 1 teaspoon chopped fresh rosemary or ¼ teaspoon dried, crushed rosemary
- 2 tablespoons light mayonnaise
- 1/8 cup chopped fresh parsley
- ½ teaspoon chopped fresh thyme or 1/8 teaspoon dried thyme

For salad sandwich:

- 1 can (4.5 - 5 ounces) white albacore tuna, well-drained
- 6 tablespoons chopped celery
- Salt to taste
- 1 cup chopped spinach
- ½ can (from a 15 ounce can) chickpeas, drained, rinsed
- 3 tablespoons finely chopped red onion
- 1 medium tomato, sliced
- 1 whole wheat pita bread, cut in half

Directions:

1. To make the dressing: combine mayonnaise, Greek yogurt, lemon juice, and herbs in a bowl.

2. To make the salad: combine celery, chickpeas, spinach, onion, and tuna in a bowl. Stir in dressing.

3. To make sandwiches: cut each half of the pita pocket in the center, horizontally (except the edges) to make pockets.

4. Fill the salad and tomatoes into the pita pockets and serve.

Egg Salad Lettuce Wraps

Number of servings: 2

Nutritional values per serving: (2 wraps with 1 cup carrot sticks)

Calories – 435

Fat – 27 grams

Carbohydrates – 21 grams

Protein – 27 grams

Ingredients:

- ½ cup nonfat Greek yogurt
- 1 teaspoon Dijon mustard or to taste
- Salt to taste
- Pepper to taste
- 4 stalks celery, minced
- 4 large iceberg lettuce leaves
- 4 carrots, peeled, cut into sticks
- 2 tablespoons mayonnaise
- Salt to taste
- 6 hard-boiled eggs, peeled,
- ¼ cup minced red onion
- 2 tablespoons chopped fresh basil

Directions:

1. Combine mayonnaise, mustard, yogurt, salt, and pepper in a bowl.
2. Cut the eggs into two halves and remove 2 yolks. These yolks are not needed.
3. Cut all the eggs into cubes. Add eggs into the bowl of mayonnaise along with onion and celery and stir until well combined.
4. Cut each lettuce leaf into two halves. Stack two halves together. You should have four stacks in total.

5. Distribute the egg salad among the lettuce stacks and scatter basil on top. Wrap and serve with carrot sticks.

Cabbage Barley Soup

Number of servings: 4

Nutritional values per serving:

Calories - 195

Fat - 1 grams

Carbohydrates - 37 grams

Protein - 11 grams

Ingredients:

- ¼ cup medium-size pearl barley
- ½ cup dried brown lentils, rinsed
- 1 ½ medium carrots, chopped
- ¼ teaspoon poultry seasoning
- 23 ounces V8 juice
- 4 cups shredded cabbage
- Salt to taste
- 1 stalk celery, chopped
- Pepper to taste
- 2 cups water
- 4 ounces fresh mushrooms, sliced

Directions:

1. Place barley, lentils, carrots, poultry seasoning, V8 juice, water, cabbage, and celery in a soup pot.
2. Place the soup pot over medium flame. When the mixture begins to boil, lower the flame and cook until lentils and barley are tender. It can take a long time to cook, so if you have an instant pot or pressure cooker, use this to make the soup. It will cook much faster.
3. Add salt, pepper, and mushroom and stir. Cover the pot and continue cooking until mushrooms are soft.
4. Ladle into soup bowls and serve.

Carolina Shrimp Soup

Number of servings: 3

Nutritional values per serving:

Calories - 190

Fat - 5 grams

Carbohydrates - 18 grams

Protein - 19 grams

Ingredients:

- 2 teaspoons olive oil, divided
- 3 cloves garlic, minced
- ½ medium sweet red pepper, cut into ¾ inch squares
- ½ can (from a 15.5 ounce can) black-eyed peas, rinsed, drained
- Pepper to taste
- ½ pound uncooked shrimp, peeled, deveined
- ½ bunch kale, trimmed, coarsely chopped (8 cups after chopping)
- 1 ½ cups chicken broth
- Salt to taste
- Finely chopped chives (optional)

Directions:

1. Pour 1 teaspoon oil into a soup pot and heat over medium-high flame. When oil is heated, place shrimp in the pan and stir until they are coated with oil.

2. Stir in garlic and cook for a couple of minutes until they are pink. Transfer the shrimp onto a plate.

3. Pour 1 teaspoon oil into the pot and let it heat. When oil is hot, add kale and red pepper and stir. Cover and cook until the vegetables are tender.

4. Pour broth. When the mixture begins to boil, add black-eyed peas, shrimp, pepper, and salt and stir.

5. Heat thoroughly. Ladle into soup bowls. Garnish with chives and serve.

Sesame Shrimp with Smashed Cucumber Salad

Number of servings: 2

Nutritional values per serving:

Calories - 235

Fat - 15 grams

Carbohydrates - 9 grams

Protein - 16 grams

Ingredients:

- 2 tablespoons toasted sesame oil, divided
- 2 ½ teaspoons low-sodium soy sauce, divided
- 1 tablespoon chopped flat-leaf parsley
- ½ tablespoon honey
- ½ teaspoon crushed red pepper
- ½ pound medium shrimp, peeled, deveined
- 1 cup thinly sliced cucumber
- 1 tablespoon rice vinegar
- ½ tablespoon minced fresh ginger
- 2 small cloves garlic, minced

Directions:

1. Pour a tablespoon of oil into a skillet and heat over medium-high flame. Add shrimp once the oil is hot. Cook for 3 minutes, flip, and cook the other side for 3 minutes.

2. Stir in 1 ½ teaspoons soy sauce and cook for about 30 seconds. Turn off the heat.

3. Pour remaining oil and soy sauce into a Ziploc bag. Also, add parsley, honey, red pepper, cucumber, rice vinegar, ginger, and garlic.

4. Seal the bag. Shake well so that the contents are well combined.

5. Place the bag on your cutting board so that it is lying flat. Roll the bag with a rolling pin. This is done to smash the cucumber slices.

6. Divide shrimp onto two plates. Divide the cucumber mixture onto the plates and serve.

Quinoa Corn Chowder

Number of servings: 4

Nutritional values per serving:

Calories - 315

Fat - 9 grams

Carbohydrates - 48 grams

Protein - 12 grams

Ingredients:

- ½ cup quinoa
- ½ medium onion, diced
- ½ teaspoon minced garlic
- ¼ teaspoon dried thyme
- ½ teaspoon dried parsley
- 2 tablespoons flour
- 1 cup milk
- ½ can (from a 15 ounce can) white kidney beans, rinsed, drained
- 1 ½ tablespoons canola oil
- ½ red pepper, diced
- Salt to taste
- 1 ½ cups chicken broth
- 2 cups fresh or frozen corn kernels

Directions:

1. Place a pot over a medium flame. Let the pot heat up. Add quinoa and toast for 2 to 3 minutes until you get a nice aroma. Keep stirring throughout.

2. Stir in oil, pepper, and onion and raise the heat to medium-high.

3. Cook until the onion turns translucent. Stir in garlic, salt, and dried herbs. Cook for about a minute or until you get a nice fragrance.

4. Add flour and stir until well incorporated. Add broth and whisk well.

5. Add milk, stirring constantly. Keep stirring until slightly thick and comes to a boil.

6. Lower the flame and cook without covering until quinoa is tender.

7. Stir in the corn and beans. Heat thoroughly.

8. Ladle into soup bowls and serve.

Oven-Fried Chicken

Number of servings: 2

Nutritional values per serving:

Calories - 320

Fat - 14 grams

Carbohydrates - 24 grams

Protein - 21 grams

Ingredients:

- ½ pound frozen chicken breasts, thawed, cut into strips
- 6 tablespoons flour
- ¼ teaspoon salt
- 1 teaspoon paprika
- ¼ teaspoon pepper
- 2 tablespoons melted butter or more if required
- ¼ cup panko breadcrumbs
- ½ tablespoon seasoning salt

Directions:

1. Line a baking tray by placing a sheet of parchment paper over it. Brush butter on the parchment paper as well.
2. Place flour, salt, pepper, paprika, breadcrumbs, and salt in a Ziploc bag. Seal the bag and shake until well combined.
3. Place chicken in the bag and seal the bag. Shake until the chicken is coated with the mixture.
4. Place the coated chicken on the baking sheet. Make sure to space out the strips.
5. Place the baking tray in an oven that has been preheated to 425°F and bake for about 10 minutes.
6. Flip the chicken over and continue baking for 10 - 15 minutes or until the chicken is cooked through and golden-brown on the outside.

7. Serve right away.

Greek Salad Wraps

Number of servings: 3

Nutritional values per serving: (1 wrap with 1 ½ cups of salad)

Calories - 335

Fat - 14 grams

Carbohydrates - 42 grams

Protein - 9 grams

Ingredients:

- 3 tablespoons red wine vinegar
- 1 tablespoon finely chopped fresh oregano
- Salt to taste
- Pepper to taste
- ½ can (from a 15 ounce can) low-sodium chickpeas, rinsed
- ½ cup halved cherry tomatoes or grape tomatoes
- 1/8 cup slivered red onion
- 2 tablespoons extra-virgin olive oil
- 4 cups chopped romaine lettuce
- ¾ cup sliced cucumbers (cut into half-moon slices)
- 1/8 cup sliced, pitted kalamata olives
- 3 whole-wheat wraps (8 - 9 inches each)

Directions:

1. Combine oil, vinegar, pepper, salt, and oregano in a large bowl. Whisk well.

2. Add all the vegetables, chickpeas, and olives and toss well.

3. Spread the wraps on a large serving plate. Divide the salad among the wraps (each portion should be 1 ½ cups).

4. Roll the wraps and place with the seam side facing down.

Snack Recipes

Mini Chicken Fajitas

Number of servings: 18

Nutritional values per serving: (1 mini fajita)

Calories – 40

Fat – 2 grams

Carbohydrates – 3 grams

Protein – 3 grams

Ingredients:

- 1 tablespoon oil of your choice
- ½ yellow bell pepper, cut into ½ inch squares
- ½ red bell pepper, cut into ½ inch squares
- 1 skinless chicken breast, cut into ½ inch squares
- ½ teaspoon ground coriander
- ½ teaspoon ground cumin
- 1/8 teaspoon chili powder or to taste
- 8 ounces canned, chopped tomatoes
- 2 green onions, thinly sliced
- 3 small flour tortillas
- 1 tablespoon chipotle paste
- A handful of fresh cilantro, chopped
- 1.5 ounces pre-grated mozzarella cheese

For guacamole:

- ½ avocado, peeled, pitted, mashed
- 2 small cloves garlic, crushed
- Juice of ½ lime or more to taste
- 1 tablespoon finely chopped fresh cilantro

Directions:

1. Pour oil into a nonstick pan and heat over medium flame. When the oil is heated, add chicken and bell peppers and cook for a couple of minutes.
2. Combine cumin, coriander, and chili powder in a bowl and sprinkle over the chicken and peppers. Stir-fry for a few more seconds.
3. Add tomatoes and chipotle paste and mix well. Cook until you get a nice and thick sauce. Make sure you stir often.
4. Add green onions and cilantro and mix well. Turn off the flame after a minute. Let cool.
5. Meanwhile, cut each tortilla into six equal triangles, so you get 18 triangles in total.
6. Take a teaspoonful of the chicken mixture and place it on the shorter end of the triangle. Place a little of the cheese over the chicken mixture.
7. Now start rolling from this side, along with the filling, till you reach the tip of the triangle. Insert a toothpick to fasten and place it on a baking tray.
8. Repeat steps 6 – 7 and make the remaining fajitas.
9. Cover the baking tray with plastic wrap and place it in the refrigerator until use.
10. Meanwhile, to make guacamole, combine avocado, garlic, lime juice, and cilantro in a bowl and stir until smooth. Cover and place in the refrigerator until use. Use the dip within two days.
11. To cook the fajitas, remove the plastic wrap and place the baking tray in an oven that has been preheated to 350°F, for about 10 minutes or until nice and hot.
12. Serve mini fajitas with guacamole.

Hummus

Number of servings: 3

Nutritional values per serving: (4 tablespoons)

Calories – 145

Fat – 9 grams

Carbohydrates – 13 grams

Protein – 3 grams

Ingredients:

- 2 small cloves garlic, peeled, smashed, finely chopped
- 1 ½ tablespoons fresh lemon juice
- ½ tablespoon tahini
- ½ can (from a 15 ounce can) chickpeas, rinsed, drained
- 1 ½ tablespoons extra-virgin olive oil
- ¼ teaspoon salt

Directions:

1. Place garlic, chickpeas, olive oil, lemon juice, salt, and tahini in the food processor bowl. Keep blending until you get a smooth puree.

2. Pour into a bowl. Cover the bowl and chill until use. It can last for five days.

3. You can serve hummus with vegetable sticks (carrots, cucumber, celery, etc.), crackers, or falafel. You can also use it with pita chips or as a filling or spread for sandwiches. You can also use it in salads.

Easy Oven Baked Falafel

Number of servings: 2

Nutritional values per serving: (3 falafels, without hummus or other serving options)

Calories – 155

Fat – 1 gram

Carbohydrates – 25 grams

Protein – 6 grams

Ingredients:
- ¾ cup cooked or canned chickpeas
- ½ cup parsley
- 2 cloves garlic, peeled
- 1 tablespoon lime juice
- ½ teaspoon sea salt
- ½ teaspoon basil
- ¼ teaspoon ground nutmeg
- ½ cup chopped cilantro
- 2 tablespoons whole-wheat flour
- ¼ red onion, finely chopped
- ½ teaspoon pepper
- ½ teaspoon ground cumin
- ½ teaspoon dried oregano

Directions:

1. Place herbs, spices, lime juice, chickpeas, garlic, and onion in the food processor bowl and process until you get a coarse mixture.

2. Add whole wheat flour and give short pulses until well combined, and you get a sticky dough.

3. Add the mixture into a bowl. Place the bowl in the refrigerator for about 30 minutes.

4. Prepare a baking tray by lining it with parchment paper. Make six equal portions of the mixture and shape them into patties.

5. Place the patties on the baking tray and put it in an oven that has been preheated to 425°F for about 30 - 40 minutes or baked until crisp and brown.

6. Serve falafel with hummus. You can also make a bigger falafel and place it in between buns with toppings of your choice to make falafel burgers. You can stuff it in pita bread along with hummus and vegetables to make sandwiches.

Apple Pie Energy Bites

Number of servings: 12

Nutritional values per serving: (2 bites)

Calories - 320

Fat - 15 grams

Carbohydrates - 39 grams

Protein - 9 g

Ingredients:

- 4 cups old fashioned rolled oats
- 4 tablespoons ground flaxseeds
- 2 tablespoons chopped hazelnuts
- 1 teaspoon ground allspice
- 2 teaspoons vanilla extract
- ½ cup unsweetened dried cranberries
- 2 teaspoons ground cinnamon
- 1 teaspoon salt
- 2 tablespoons chopped walnuts
- 1 cup almond butter
- 4 tablespoons honey
- 2 cups grated Granny Smith apples
- 2 teaspoons lemon juice

Directions:

1. Place apples in a bowl. Drizzle lemon juice all over and toss well.
2. Combine oats, flaxseeds, cinnamon, salt, nuts, and allspice in another bowl.
3. Combine honey, vanilla, and almond butter in a third bowl.
4. Pour the honey mixture into the bowl of oats and stir until well incorporated.

5. Add apples and cranberries and stir until well incorporated.

6. Divide the mixture into 24 equal portions and shape into balls. Place the balls in an airtight container and chill until use. It can last for 4 days.

Chipotle Black Bean Dip with Corn Chips

Number of servings: 3

Nutritional values per serving: (6 tortilla chips with ¼ cup dip)

Calories – 145

Fat – 3.5 grams

Carbohydrates – 28 grams

Protein – 6.5 grams

Ingredients:

- 3 corn tortillas (6 inches each), cut each into 6 equal wedges
- ½ teaspoon olive oil
- ½ teaspoon cumin seeds
- Salt to taste
- ½ cup chopped onions
- 2 small cloves garlic, minced
- ½ can (from a 15 ounce can) black beans, with its liquid
- 1 tablespoon crumbled queso fresco cheese
- ½ chipotle chili in adobo sauce
- A large pinch dried oregano
- ½ ounce shredded part-skim mozzarella cheese
- 3 tablespoons unsalted, canned, diced tomatoes with its liquid

Directions:

1. Take a baking tray and cover with a sheet of parchment paper, and grease it with cooking spray. Place wedges on the baking sheet. Season with salt.

2. Place the baking tray in an oven that has been preheated to 400°F and bake for about 10 minutes or until crisp and brown. Make sure to flip the tortilla chips halfway through baking.

3. While the chips are baking, pour oil into a saucepan and place the saucepan over medium flame.

4. When the oil is heated, add onion and cook until translucent. Stir in cumin and garlic and sauté for a minute or until you get a nice aroma.

5. Stir in beans and oregano and mash well using a potato masher.

6. Lower the flame and cook until thick. Turn off the flame.

7. Grease a small baking dish with cooking spray. Spread the bean mixture into the baking dish.

8. Sprinkle queso fresco and mozzarella cheese on top. Place the baking dish in the oven and bake for a few minutes until cheese melts and is bubbling.

9. Blend together tomatoes and chipotle chili into a blender until you get a smooth puree.

10. Pour the tomato mixture over the cheese layer. Garnish with cilantro and serve with corn chips.

Almond Poppy Crackers

Number of servings: 40

Nutritional values per serving: (1 cracker)

Calories - 60

Fat - 5 grams

Carbohydrates - 2 grams

Protein - 2 grams

Ingredients:

- 3 cups almond flour
- 2 tablespoons olive oil
- 2 large egg whites
- 2 tablespoons poppy seeds
- 2 teaspoons fine grain salt

Directions:

1. Prepare two baking trays by lining them with parchment paper. Keep rack in the center of the oven. Set the temperature of the oven to 350°F and preheat the oven.
2. Place almond flour, salt, and poppy seeds in a bowl and stir until well combined.
3. Stir in oil and egg whites. Mix until a dough is formed. Divide the dough into 2 equal portions and shape it into balls.
4. Place a dough ball on the center of the baking tray. Place another sheet of parchment paper on top of the dough. Roll with a rolling pin, giving the shape of an 8 x 12 inches rectangle.
5. Gently remove the top parchment paper. Cut into 20 equal rectangles. Do not separate the crackers yet.
6. Repeat steps 4 - 5 and make the remaining crackers.
7. Bake the crackers in batches.

8. Place the baking sheet in an oven that has been preheated to 350°F for about 12 - 14 minutes or until crisp and brown. Keep watch over the crackers after 12 minutes of baking as they can burn easily.

9. Let cool completely. You can now separate the crackers by either breaking them apart or cutting them once again on the marked rectangles.

10. Transfer the crackers into an airtight container. It can last for a week. You can serve the crackers as is or with a dip or toppings of your choice.

Frozen Berry Yogurt

Number of servings: 2

Nutritional values per serving:

Calories - 70

Fat - 0 grams

Carbohydrates - 10 grams

Protein - 7 grams

Ingredients:
- 4.4 ounces frozen mixed berries
- ½ tablespoon honey or agave nectar
- 4.4 ounces nonfat Greek yogurt

Directions:

1. Place berries in the food processor bowl along with honey and yogurt. Blend until you get a soft-serve texture.

2. Serve in bowls right away.

Turkey Pesto Roll-Up

Number of servings: 4

Nutritional values per serving: (3 rolls)

Calories - 165

Fat - 7.5 grams

Carbohydrates - 11.5 grams

Protein - 12 grams

Ingredients:

- 2 cucumbers (about 6 - 7 inches long), trimmed, unpeeled
- 2 ounces cheddar cheese (6 thin slices)
- 2 red bell peppers, cut into matchsticks
- 4 ounces deli turkey (6 thin slices)
- 2 tablespoons pesto or more if required
- Pepper to taste
- 2 cups greens of your choice
- Salt and pepper to taste

Directions:

1. Cut the cucumbers into thin slices with a mandoline slicer or a sharp knife. You should get about six slices from each cucumber.
2. Spread pesto lightly on the cucumber slices. Place turkey slices and cheese slices over the cucumber slices. Sprinkle with salt and pepper. Spread the thin bell pepper slices and greens over the cheese.
3. Roll the cucumber slices and fasten with a toothpick.
4. Serve.

Tomato Basil Soup

Number of servings: 6

Nutritional values per serving:

Calories – 80

Fat – 4 grams

Carbohydrates – 9 grams

Protein – 3 grams

Ingredients:

- 4 teaspoons olive oil
- 2 stalks celery, finely chopped
- 1 cup chopped fresh basil
- 4 cans (14 ounces each) diced tomatoes, unsalted
- 2 small onions, finely chopped
- 2 cloves garlic, peeled, minced
- 2 teaspoons chopped fresh thyme
- Salt to taste
- 4 cups vegetable broth or chicken broth
- Pepper to taste

Directions:

1. Pour oil into a soup pot and place it over medium flame. When the oil is heated, add onion, garlic, and celery and cook until slightly tender. Make sure that the garlic does not turn brown.
2. Stir in the herbs, broth, and tomatoes. When it starts to boil, lower the flame and cook for about 15 minutes, stirring every 5 minutes. Turn off the flame and let it cool.
3. Blend the soup using an immersion blender until smooth or to the desired consistency. You can use a regular blender.
4. Serve the soup hot, warm, or chilled.

Zucchini Feta Fritters

Number of servings: 4

Nutritional values per serving: (3 fritters)

Calories – 240

Fat – 9 grams

Carbohydrates – 24 grams

Protein – 17 grams

Ingredients:

- 2 pounds zucchini, trimmed, peeled, shredded
- ½ cup finely chopped parsley
- ½ cup finely chopped dill
- 2 eggs
- Salt to taste
- 1 cup feta cheese crumbles
- 2 jalapeño peppers, diced
- ½ cup flour or more if required
- Pepper to taste

Directions:

1. Place zucchini on a large cheesecloth. Bring the edges together and squeeze out the moisture, removing as much as possible.
2. Place zucchini, parsley, dill, eggs, salt, feta cheese, jalapeño peppers, flour, and pepper in a bowl and mix until well combined. If the mixture is watery, add more flour and mix well.
3. Divide the mixture into 12 equal portions and form it into patties.
4. Place a large nonstick pan over a medium flame. Spray the pan with cooking spray. Place fritters in the pan (as many as can fit) and fry the remaining in batches.

5. Cook until the underside is golden brown. Flip the fritters over and cook the other side until golden brown.

6. Remove the fritters from the pan and place them on a plate.

7. Cook the remaining fritters similarly.

8. Serve fritters with tzatziki or yogurt sauce. The recipe of tzatziki follows in the next recipe (Mediterranean meatballs gyro sandwich).

Dinner Recipes

Mediterranean Meatballs Gyro Sandwich

Number of servings: 2

Nutritional values per serving:

Calories – 345

Fat – 14.5 grams

Carbohydrates – 21 grams

Protein – 31 grams

Ingredients:

For tzatziki sauce:

- ½ cup Greek yogurt
- ½ teaspoon finely minced garlic
- ½ tablespoon finely chopped fresh dill
- 1/8 teaspoon freshly cracked black pepper
- 1/8 cup grated English cucumber
- ½ teaspoon extra-virgin olive oil
- Sea salt to taste
- ½ tablespoon fresh lemon juice

For Mediterranean meatballs:

- 1/8 cup crushed pork rinds
- 1 tablespoon chopped, fresh flat-leaf parsley
- ¼ teaspoon ground cumin
- Freshly cracked pepper
- 1 small egg
- ½ tablespoon finely minced garlic
- ¼ teaspoon sea salt or to taste
- ½ pound ground chuck

For salad:
- ½ cup finely diced tomatoes
- ½ tablespoon finely chopped flat-leaf parsley
- ½ cup finely diced English cucumber
- Salt to taste
- ¼ cup finely chopped red onion
- Pepper to taste

To assemble:
- 2 flatbreads
- A handful of chopped parsley to garnish
- Crumbled feta cheese (optional)

Directions:

1. To make tzatziki sauce: Place yogurt, garlic, cucumber, dill, oil, pepper, lemon juice, and salt in a bowl and stir until well combined.

2. Cover the bowl and chill in the fridge until use.

3. Place a rack on a baking tray. Spray cooking spray on the rack.

4. Set the oven temperature to 425°F to preheat.

5. To make Mediterranean meatballs: mix together the pork rinds, raw egg, parsley, cumin, garlic, salt, and pepper in a bowl.

6. Add the meat and mix by hand until well combined. Make sure you do not over-mix, or else the meat will become tough.

7. Make eight equal meatballs of the mixture and place them on the rack.

8. Place the rack along with the baking tray in the oven and bake for 10 – 15 minutes or until well-cooked inside. There should be no pink in the middle. Let the meatballs rest on your countertop for 5 minutes.

9. To make the salad: combine tomatoes, cucumber, parsley, and onions in a bowl. Season with salt and pepper.

10. To assemble the sandwich: set up the oven to broil mode. Take a baking sheet and keep the flatbreads on it.

11. Place baking sheet in the oven and broil for a few minutes until toasted lightly. Turn the flatbreads over and broil for a couple of minutes until toasted lightly.

12. To assemble: place four meatballs along the diameter of each flatbread. Spread tzatziki sauce around the meatballs. Be generous with the tzatziki.

13. Scatter the salad over the meatballs. Sprinkle parsley and feta cheese. Roll the flatbreads and place on a serving plate with the seam side down, then serve.

Turkey Chili

Number of servings: 3

Nutritional values per serving: (1-½ cups, without serving options)

Calories - 335

Fat - 4 grams

Carbohydrates - 46 grams

Protein - 32 grams

Ingredients:
- 1 teaspoon olive oil
- 2 cloves garlic, minced
- ½ pound extra-lean (99%) ground turkey or chicken
- 1 teaspoon ground cumin
- 1/8 teaspoon cayenne pepper
- 2 tablespoons chili powder
- ½ teaspoon dried oregano
- Salt to taste
- ¾ cup chicken broth
- ½ can (from a 15 ounce can) sweet corn, rinsed, drained
- ½ can (from a 28 ounce can) diced tomatoes or crushed tomatoes
- ½ red bell pepper, diced
- 1 can (15 ounce can) dark red kidney beans, rinsed, and drained

Optional toppings:
- Grated cheese
- Tortilla chips
- Sour cream
- Chopped cilantro

- Chopped avocado
- Any other toppings of your choice

Directions:

1. Pour oil into a soup pot and place it over medium-high flame. When the oil is heated, add garlic, onion, and red bell pepper and cook for a few minutes until slightly tender.

2. Stir in turkey. Cook until the meat is light brown. As you stir, break down the turkey into smaller pieces.

3. Stir in the spices, salt, and oregano, and cook for a few seconds until you get a nice aroma.

4. Stir in tomatoes, kidney beans, broth, and corn. When it begins to boil, lower the flame and cook until thick. Stir occasionally.

5. Taste the chili and adjust seasoning as required.

6. Ladle into bowls. Serve with any of the suggested serving options.

Chicken Chow Mein

Number of servings: 3

Nutritional values per serving:

Calories - 390

Fat - 5 grams

Carbohydrates - 59 grams

Protein - 24 grams

Ingredients:
- ½ tablespoon canola oil
- ½ red bell pepper, diced
- 1 ½ cups shredded cabbage or coleslaw mix
- ½ teaspoon minced garlic
- A pinch of red pepper flakes
- 2 tablespoons soy sauce
- 6.6 ounces whole-wheat spaghetti
- ½ tablespoon cornstarch mixed with a tablespoon of water (optional)
- 1 ½ chicken breasts, skinless, boneless, cut into cubes
- ½ cup stringed snap peas
- 1 large carrot, peeled, shredded
- ¼ teaspoon minced ginger
- 2 cups chicken broth
- 2 tablespoons hoisin sauce

Directions:

1. Place a pot over a medium-high flame. Add oil and let it heat. Once the oil is heated, add chicken and cook until brown.

2. Stir in peas, red pepper, carrot, and cabbage, and cook until slightly tender.

3. Stir in ginger, garlic, and red pepper flakes. Cook for a few seconds until you get a nice aroma.

4. Pour soy sauce, broth, and hoisin sauce and mix well. When the mixture begins to boil, lower the heat to medium and add in the pasta.

5. Stir often and cook until nearly dry. Now cover the pot and continue cooking for a couple of minutes or until pasta is cooked.

6. Add cornstarch mixture if desired and constantly stir until thick.

7. Serve hot.

Chicken Tortilla Soup

Number of servings: 4

Nutritional values per serving:

Calories - 200

Fat - 8 grams

Carbohydrates - 9 grams

Protein - 22 grams

Ingredients:

- 1 tablespoon olive oil
- ½ can (from a 4 ounce can) chopped green chilies
- ½ jalapeño, chopped
- ½ can (from a 15 ounce can) tomato sauce
- 2 ½ cups low sodium chicken broth
- 2 tablespoons minced cilantro
- Salt to taste
- Pepper to taste
- ½ large onion, chopped
- 1 clove garlic, minced
- ½ teaspoon ground cumin
- ½ can (from a 14.5 ounce can) diced tomatoes with garlic and onion, with its liquid
- ½ rotisserie chicken, shredded, skinless
- 1 teaspoon lime juice
- Shredded Monterey Jack or sharp cheddar cheese to serve
- Crushed tortilla chips to serve

Directions:

1. Place a Dutch oven over medium flame. Add oil and let it heat. Add onions once the oil is hot and cook until they turn soft.

2. Stir in garlic, chili, cumin, and jalapeño. Stir constantly for about a minute or until you get a nice aroma.

3. Add tomatoes, tomato sauce, and broth. Stir well and wait for it to come to a boil.

4. Lower the flame and add chicken. Mix well. Cook for about 7 – 8 minutes.

5. Stir in lime juice, cilantro, salt, and pepper.

6. Ladle into soup bowls. Garnish with tortilla chips, cheese, and serve.

Maple Glazed Salmon

Number of servings: 2

Nutritional values per serving: (1 fillet)

Calories - 270

Fat - 9.5 grams

Carbohydrates - 7 grams

Protein - 36 grams

Ingredients:

- 2 skinless salmon fillets (6 ounces each)
- ¼ - ½ teaspoon garlic powder
- ¼ teaspoon smoked paprika
- ¼ teaspoon salt
- A pinch of ground red pepper
- Lemon juice to drizzle

Directions:

1. Set the oven to broil mode and preheat the oven to high heat. Prepare a baking tray by lining it with aluminum foil. Spray cooking spray over the foil.
2. Mix salt and all the spices in a bowl. Sprinkle spice mixture all over the fillets and place them on the baking tray.
3. Place baking tray in the oven. Set the timer for 5 minutes and let the fillets broil.
4. Brush maple syrup over the fillets and broil for another minute or until the fish is the way you like it cooked (ideal temperature for salmon is medium-rare to medium).
5. Squeeze lemon juice on top and serve.

Vegetarian Bourguignon

Number of servings: 2 - 3

Nutritional values per serving: (1 cup)

Calories - 270

Fat - 10 grams

Carbohydrates - 23 grams

Protein - 4 grams

Ingredients:

- 1 ½ tablespoons butter, divided
- 1 stalk celery, sliced
- ½ cup chopped carrots (½ inch pieces)
- ½ large shallot, minced
- 2 small bay leaves
- ½ cup chopped parsnip (½ inch pieces)
- ½ pound mixed mushrooms, halved
- 2 small cloves garlic, minced
- ½ tablespoon extra-virgin olive oil
- ¼ teaspoon dried thyme
- Salt to taste
- Pepper to taste
- ½ tablespoon all-purpose flour
- 2 tablespoons cognac or brandy
- ¾ cup frozen pearl onions, thawed
- 1 tablespoon tomato paste
- ¾ cup dry red wine
- ¾ cup vegetable broth or mushroom broth

Directions:

1. Place a pot over a medium-high flame. Add 1 tablespoon of butter and ½ a tablespoon of oil. When the butter melts, stir in the parsnip, celery, and carrot and cook until the veggies are slightly tender.
2. Lower the heat to medium and stir in the shallot, mushrooms, bay leaves, salt, garlic, thyme, and pepper, and cook until the mushrooms are soft.
3. Add tomato paste and mix well. Scatter flour on top and constantly stir for about 30 seconds.
4. Pour wine and cognac and stir. Raise to medium-high heat and scrape the bottom of the pot to remove any particles that may be stuck. When the liquid in the pot reduces to half its original quantity, stir in the broth.
5. When the mixture begins to boil, lower the flame once again and cover the pot partially. Let it simmer until the vegetables are slightly soft.
6. Add pearl onions and stir. Continue cooking for another 4 - 5 minutes.
7. Turn off the heat. Add ½ a tablespoon of butter, salt, and pepper and stir.
8. Serve hot.

Vegetarian Enchilada Casserole

Number of servings: 4

Nutritional values per serving: (1 ½ cups)

Calories - 360

Fat - 17 grams

Carbohydrates - 42 grams

Protein - 14 grams

Ingredients:

- 1 tablespoon extra-virgin olive oil
- 6 tablespoons chopped poblano peppers
- ½ medium zucchini halved lengthwise, cut into ¼ inch thick half moons
- ½ medium yellow squash halved lengthwise, cut into ¼ inch half moons
- ½ cup chopped onion
- 3 cloves garlic, minced
- ½ cup fresh corn kernels
- ¼ teaspoon salt or to taste
- ½ can (from a 15 ounce can) unsalted black beans, rinsed
- ½ can (from a 15 ounce can) unsalted pinto beans, rinsed
- 4 corn tortillas (6 inches each)
- ½ avocado, peeled, pitted, diced
- ¼ cup low-fat sour cream
- ½ cup Pico de Gallo
- ¼ teaspoon salt or to taste
- ¾ cup shredded pepper Jack cheese
- ¼ cup sliced scallions

Directions:

1. Pour oil into a skillet and heat over medium-high flame. When the oil is heated, add onion, garlic, and poblano peppers and cook for a few minutes.
2. When the onion turns pink, stir in zucchini, squash, Pico de Gallo, corn, and salt. Cook until slightly thick.
3. Turn off the heat. Add pinto and black beans. Stir until well combined.
4. Grease a small baking dish or casserole dish with cooking spray.
5. Spread 1/3 of the bean mixture into the baking dish.
6. Spread two tortillas over the bean mixture. If needed, tear the tortillas to fit into the dish.
7. Repeat steps 5 - 6. Spread the remaining bean mixture over the tortillas. Finally, top with cheese.
8. Set the oven temperature to 350°F to preheat. Place the baking dish in the oven and bake for about 20 - 25 minutes until heated thoroughly and the cheese melts.
9. Garnish with sour cream, scallions, and avocado.
10. Serve.

Ham and Pineapple Rice

Number of servings: 2

Nutritional values per serving:

Calories - 330

Fat - 3 grams

Carbohydrates - 60 grams

Protein - 17 grams

Ingredients:

- 1 cup cooked, chopped ham
- ½ can (from a 13.2 ounce can) pineapple tidbits, drained but retaining the juice
- 1 tablespoon soy sauce
- ¼ teaspoon salt or to taste
- 1 green onion, sliced
- ¾ cup low-sodium chicken broth
- ½ tablespoon Worcestershire sauce
- ½ cup long-grain white or brown rice rinsed well
- ¼ cup pineapple juice or more if required (use the juice from the canned pineapple)

Directions:

1. Place ham, pineapple juice, Worcestershire sauce, soy sauce, broth, and salt in a skillet. Place the skillet over high flame.

2. When the mixture begins to boil, add raw rice and stir. Lower the heat to medium-low. Cook covered until dry. If the rice looks uncooked, add more of the pineapple juice and simmer until rice is cooked.

3. Add green onions, stir, and serve.

Skillet Chicken Parmesan

Number of servings: 2

Nutritional values per serving:

Calories - 440

Fat - 24 grams

Carbohydrates - 11 grams

Protein - 46 grams

Ingredients:

- 2 boneless, skinless chicken breasts
- Salt to taste
- ½ teaspoon minced garlic
- ½ teaspoon dried oregano
- ½ teaspoon dried parsley
- Pepper to taste
- ½ can (from a 28 ounce can) crushed tomatoes
- ½ teaspoon sugar (optional)
- ¼ cup shredded parmesan cheese
- ¼ cup shredded mozzarella cheese
- 1 tablespoon canola oil
- 1 small onion, chopped

Directions:

1. Pour oil into a skillet and place the skillet over a medium flame. Let the oil heat.

2. Season chicken with salt and pepper and place in the skillet.

3. Cook until golden brown all over and well-cooked inside.

4. Remove chicken from the pan and place it on a plate to rest. Keep the plate covered with aluminum foil.

5. Add onion into the skillet and cook until soft. Stir in the garlic and herbs. Cook for about a minute or until you get a nice aroma.

6. Throw in the salt, tomatoes, and sugar. Cook over medium-low flame for about 5 minutes.

7. Place the chicken back in the pan and stir. Heat thoroughly. Turn off the heat. Sprinkle cheese on top and cover the pan with a lid for a few minutes until the cheese melts.

8. Serve.

Skillet Lasagna

Number of servings: 10

Nutritional values per serving:

Calories – 430

Fat – 9 grams

Carbohydrates – 51 grams

Protein – 38 grams

Ingredients:

- 2 pounds ground turkey or chicken or lean ground beef
- 1 onion, finely chopped
- 2 small zucchinis, trimmed, shredded
- 2 bell peppers, chopped
- 2 large carrots, shredded
- Pepper to taste
- Salt to taste
- 2 teaspoons Italian seasoning
- Red pepper flakes to taste
- 6 cups low-sodium chicken broth
- 2 cups shredded mozzarella cheese
- 2 cans (14 ounces each) crushed tomatoes
- 17.5 ounces dry lasagna sheets

Directions:

1. Place a skillet over a medium flame. Add turkey and cook until light brown. Break the meat as it cooks.

2. Stir in the onion and pepper. Once the turkey turns brown, stir in the zucchini, carrots, and spices.

3. Add in the broth and tomatoes and mix well. Add the lasagna sheets into the skillet and place them in layers with turkey and vegetables between each one, making sure the lasagna is coated by the broth and tomatoes.

4. Increase the heat to medium-high and cook until the pasta is al dente. Turn off the heat.

5. Garnish with cheese and cover the pot. Let it rest for 5 minutes. Serve right away.

Sample Meal Plan

Now that you are armed with all the recipes you need to follow the 16/8 intermittent fasting protocol, it is time to create a meal plan. Here is a sample meal plan that you can use for inspiration:

Day 1

Breakfast: Peanut butter cup shake.

Lunch: Green goddess salad with chicken.

Dinner: Skillet Chicken Parmesan.

Day 2

Breakfast: Veggie mini quiches.

Lunch: Black bean and mango salad.

Dinner: Maple-glazed salmon.

Day 3

Breakfast: Dark chocolate peppermint shake.

Lunch: Tuna and chickpea pita sandwiches.

Dinner: Vegetarian bourguignon.

Day 4

Breakfast: Ham, egg, and avocado breakfast burrito.

Lunch: Cucumber turkey club sandwiches.

Dinner: Chicken tortilla soup.

Day 5

Breakfast: Very berry super shake.

Lunch: Egg salad lettuce wraps.

Dinner: Chicken chow mein.

Day 6

Breakfast: Cauliflower English muffins.

Lunch: Cabbage barley soup.

Dinner: Turkey chili.

Day 7

Breakfast: Summer skillet vegetables and egg scramble.

Lunch: Carolina shrimp soup.

Dinner: Mediterranean meatballs gyro sandwich.

Conclusion

Ultimately, intermittent fasting is incredibly simple. The 16/8 protocol suggests you need to fast for sixteen hours a day, with an eating window restricted to only eight hours. Depending on your needs and requirements, you can easily accommodate several meals and snacks within this timeframe. All your nutritional requirements can be fulfilled without compromising taste. Also, since intermittent fasting doesn't explicitly exclude any food groups, you can add various meals to your daily diet.

Don't forget to include some form of physical activity in your daily schedule if you want to enhance and maintain the benefits of intermittent fasting. Whether weight loss is your priority or you want to improve your overall health, this diet has something to offer for everyone. Since it is perfectly sustainable, you can reap all the benefits it has to offer in weeks. By following the simple advice and suggestions given in this book, transitioning into this form of eating becomes easy. While making a dietary change, make sure you are mentally and physically ready for it. Don't hesitate to use the intermittent fasting tips, strategies, and suggestions in this book to maximize your chances of success.

Before you jump headfirst into this diet, make sure you know why you are doing it. This motivation will help you to overcome any setbacks you face while fasting.

So, what are you waiting for? All that's left is to create an action plan and get going. By simply paying attention to when you eat, you can improve your overall health and wellbeing. The key to good health lies in your hands. Don't forget to stock your pantry with all the required ingredients to cook delicious, healthy, and filling intermittent fasting recipes. Coupled with a helpful meal plan, this will make following the diet quite simple. Once you get into the groove of intermittent fasting, and with a good dose of perseverance and determination, you will notice substantial improvements in your overall health and wellbeing!

Here's another book by Daron McClain that you might like

References

"Can You Boost Your Metabolism?" Mayo Clinic, 2017, www.mayoclinic.org/healthy-lifestyle/weight-loss/in-depth/metabolism/art-20046508.

"Healthline: Medical Information and Health Advice You Can Trust." Healthline.com, 2000, www.healthline.com/.

https://www.facebook.com/WebMD. "Do Men Lose Weight Faster than Women?" WebMD, WebMD, 13 Oct. 2015, www.webmd.com/diet/features/do-men-lose-weight-faster-than-women#1.

NCBI. "National Center for Biotechnology Information." Nih.gov, 2019, www.ncbi.nlm.nih.gov/.

PubMed Labs. "PubMed Labs." PubMed Labs, 2019, pubmed.ncbi.nlm.nih.gov/.

Shiffer, Emily. "12 Reasons You're Not Losing Weight While Doing Intermittent Fasting, according to an RD." Women's Health, 24 Mar. 2020, www.womenshealthmag.com/weight-loss/a31816703/not-losing-weight-intermittent-fasting/.

www.ingramcontent.com/pod-product-compliance
Lightning Source LLC
LaVergne TN
LVHW051916060526
838200LV00004B/170